PROVERBS

A VERSE-BY-VERSE GUIDE TO THE
BIBLE'S BOOK OF WISDOM

PROVERBS

A VERSE-BY-VERSE GUIDE TO THE BIBLE'S BOOK OF WISDOM

TOM MEYER

ICR
INSTITUTE
FOR CREATION
RESEARCH

Dallas, Texas
ICR.org

Proverbs
A Verse-by-Verse Guide to the
Bible's Book of Wisdom

First printing: March 2022
Second printing: June 2022

Unless otherwise specified, all Scripture quotations are from the King James Version.

ISBN: 978-1-946246-73-8
Library of Congress Catalog Number: 2022930984

Please visit our website for other books and resources: ICR.org

Printed in the United States of America.

"A word fitly spoken is like apples of gold in pictures of silver."
(Proverbs 25:11)

TABLE OF CONTENTS

LIST OF TERMS

ANE .... ancient Near East

LXX.............. Septuagint

Sirach........... also known as Ecclesaisticus, an apocryphal book of wisdom

Torah............ the first five books of the Hebrew Bible

YHWH .... the covenant name for the God of Israel

INTRODUCTION

When I finished my B.A. in Bible and Theology from Shasta Bible College in Redding, California, my principal goal was to continue my journey of moving from immaturity to maturity in my knowledge of God's Word. So, after much prayer, God made it evident that a door was open for me to study in the Holy Land. At that time I wasn't married with children, so I could really give all of myself to such an immense challenge.

During the next 1,000 days I earned two M.A. degrees from Jerusalem University College on Mount Zion. While immersed in the world of the Bible, I could strive to understand through the original languages, the daily life settings, the customs and mannerisms that still exist to this day, etc., what the authors of Scripture intended to write to the original audience. For example, whenever I had a question of what a place mentioned in the Bible looked like, I physically went there. Or if I had a question on how the rabbis would understand a verse, I would simply walk down Mount Zion and ask them.

This unique opportunity to immerse oneself in the Holy Land for so long is something that cannot be replicated anywhere else in the world. There is nothing like being on location. That experience, coupled with the fact that I have 20 complete books of the Bible memorized, provides me a unique lens through which to understand Scripture, a benefit that can be enjoyed by you, your children, and your grandchildren as you read this commentary.

My primary goal in this book is to find just the right words to explain the meaning of every verse in the book of Proverbs so you and your family can continue your journey of moving from immaturity to maturity in your knowledge of God's Word.

PROVERBS 1

[1] The proverbs of Solomon the son of David, king of Israel;

In Hebrew, the title for this book is *Sefer Mishle*. *Sefer* means book. *Mashal*, meaning proverb, comes from a root meaning "to be like" or "to represent," which is fitting since many proverbs use comparisons to teach their truths. The English title *Proverbs* comes from the transliteration of the Latin Vulgate *proverbia*. The first appearance of the word *mashal* in the Bible is in Numbers 21:27 within the context of Israel's defeat of Sihon, king of the Amorites. The first citation of a proverb in the Bible is from 1 Samuel 10:12: "Therefore it became a proverb: 'is Saul also among the prophets?'" And there are over 20 New Testament quotes from the book of Proverbs. During the earliest phases of ancient Israelite society, power rested in tribal elders, who perpetuated their authority through legal statutes and traditional sayings. Clearly established and beyond dispute, laws compelled obedience insofar as they voiced the will of respected figures, whose wide experience, fairness, and good judgment set them apart from ordinary citizens as custodians of Israelite tradition. In a similar way, proverbial sayings carried the weight of experience, embodying a way of life that was binding on everyone but rebels who questioned the fundamental basis of society. This law and tradition constituted ancient Israel's attempt to establish and maintain order in complex human relationships. Of over 900 proverbs in this book, most are attributed to Solomon, so he is ascribed as the primary author of the book, as the opening verses state. Solomon was renowned for speaking 3,000 proverbs (1 Kings 4:32). It appears that many of his noteworthy proverbs were assembled in a recognized codex during King Hezekiah's reign (25:1).

[2] To know wisdom and instruction; to perceive the words of understanding;

The teacher's objectives, outlined in verses 2-6, are cultivation of the mind and training in ethical principles by the use of different methods: proverbs, warnings, sayings of the sages, riddles, and puzzling questions. The teacher's primary goal is to teach wisdom and discipline through daily life settings so that the reader can understand the insights of the wise and move from immaturity to maturity.

[3] To receive the instruction of wisdom, justice, and judgment, and equity;

Continuing the purpose of the proverbs, the author states that it is to teach people to live disciplined and successful lives, to help them through wisdom (or better yet, thoughtfulness), and to do what is right, just, and fair; these three are a cluster of synonyms for wisdom, the main subject of the book.

[4] To give subtilty to the simple, to the young man knowledge and discretion.

Continuing the purpose of the book, the author states that it is also to give insight to the simple, or literally "those who are open"—open to the influences of godliness but also susceptible to ungodliness. The student is the young man; the Hebrew word for young man, *na`ar*, is used of any age from birth (Exodus 2:6) to early manhood (Genesis 34:19). He is to receive knowledge and discernment as well.

[5] A wise man will hear, and will increase learning; and a man of understanding shall attain unto wise counsels:

The wise counsels are not just for the inexperienced young men, open to the influences of the world, but also for the experienced wise man to hear or obey. The word for wise counsels in Hebrew, *tachbulah*, is related to the word "rope." As a newly planted tree may require staking for strengthening and guiding, so, in like manner, the proverbs will also help guide the wise.

[6] To understand a proverb, and the interpretation; the words of the wise, and their dark sayings.

The aim of the book is for the reader to understand the proverbs and parables, the sayings and riddles of the wise, in order to grow from immaturity to maturity. The word for dark sayings in Hebrew is "knots" and has the idea of a riddle which is difficult to untangle. Finding the right answers to the problems life presents often demands more wisdom than the average person has, hence the reason for this book.

[7] The fear of the LORD is the beginning of knowledge: but fools despise wisdom and instruction.

The first discourse or set of teachings in the book is prefaced with this verse. It is the teacher's basic theme and the motto of the book, the essence of ancient Israelite philosophy: the first step toward knowledge is having a reverential fear of YHWH.* Everything one does proves or disproves their relationship with or fear of YHWH. The first discourse (1:7-19) of the first book (1:1–9:18) is a passionate plea against being an accomplice to theft.

[8] My son, hear the instruction of thy father, and forsake not the law of thy mother:

This first discourse gives parental advice to children. Both parents in the world of the Bible were responsible for training and teaching their children. The chief literary device is that of a father speaking to a son, thus reinforcing a philosophy or ideology, the code of the family. A

---

*YHWH is the transliteration of the Hebrew name for the covenant God of Israel. It is rendered as "LORD" in some English translations.

mother's voice, although less audible in the patriarchal dominant society, gives additional weight to the warnings against foolish behavior.

[9] For they shall be an ornament of grace unto thy head, and chains about thy neck.

What the young man heeds from his wise parents will enable him not to shame his parents but to overcome folly and thus be marked with distinction in his conservative, tight-knit, and slow-paced society. This honor will be comparable to a gold crown and golden chain, like those worn by Joseph (Genesis 41:42) and Daniel (Daniel 5:29), displayed around the neck for all to admire.

[10] My son, if sinners entice thee, consent thou not.

The reader is spoken to as a son who must choose between those values that preserve society and alternative values and actions that undercut family stability and destroy the fabric of society. The father warns the son not to fall into the trap of peer pressure but to turn his back on his foolish companions and live.

[11] If they say, Come with us, let us lay wait for blood, let us lurk privily for the innocent without cause:

The father warns his son against the details of their enticement, perhaps referencing taking part in raiding and pillaging, a crime with which ancient Israel and its neighbors were all too familiar (Judges 6:5). These raiders would invade a region whenever there was an opportunity, perhaps during a period of weakened government or during a harvest when there was more to take.

[12] Let us swallow them up alive as the grave; and whole, as those that go down into the pit:

Expanding the plot of the previous verse, the objective of the foolish companions was to leave no witnesses or evidence of their evil doings and greed for gain, just as the earth swallowed up Korah, Dathan, and Abiram alive (Numbers 16:30-33).

[13] We shall find all precious substance, we shall fill our houses with spoil:

This verse continues the proposal of the foolish companions, taking it one step further. Different dangers threaten young men, but two stand out here: the encouragement from friends to unite in an endeavor to get rich quickly through criminal activity, and the seductive invitation to sensual pleasure from illicit sources.

[14] Cast in thy lot among us; let us all have one purse:

This verse is the climax of the ungodly invitation. The son faces a choice of allegiance: whether to honor his father and mother and contribute to a godly society or to join the ranks of society's dissidents and perpetuate the disintegration of his culture.

[15] My son, walk not thou in the way with them; refrain thy foot from their path:

Here the father addresses the son, who will likely be propositioned to commit such evil. Of course, in the male-dominant patriarchal society of the world of the Bible, daughters normally did not have the freedom to make decisions as sons did, hence the address is only to sons in the book.

[16] For their feet run to evil, and make haste to shed blood.

The father implores his son to choose wisely one of two paths which he can walk down: the path that leads to life or the path that leads to death (Isaiah 59:7, Romans 3:15). The two-paths motif is reminiscent of the author's father, David, who similarly presented the two ways of life in Psalm 1. The first reason to avoid being companions with evil men is the terrible extremes wicked men will go to in order to fulfill their lusts.

[17] Surely in vain the net is spread in the sight of any bird.

Nets are mostly used in the contexts of hunting and fishing in the Bible. Most of the Old Testament references to nets or traps are symbolic of spiritual or moral entrapment, as in this case. The second reason the father dissuades the son from fellowshipping with evil men is their unbridled audacity, which flies in the face of judgment.

[18] And they lay wait for their own blood; they lurk privily for their own lives.

In continuing to warn the son, the teacher uses the example of a bird who sees a trap being set and knows to stay away; this animal is wiser than the fools who set an ambush for themselves as they hastily fly into the trap of getting rich quick through immoral means. The next argument for avoiding such companions is their ultimate demise; the criminal will be caught.

[19] So are the ways of every one that is greedy of gain; which taketh away the life of the owners thereof.

In this conclusion of the first discourse (1:7-19), the teacher warns the son that covetousness or greed for gain eventually entraps the man whose heart is given to this vice and causes him to pay the ultimate price.

[20] Wisdom crieth without; she uttereth her voice in the streets:

The second discourse (1:20-33) of the first book (1:1–9:18) is the voice of wisdom coming to the assistance of the father, openly inviting young men to hearken to and obey her words. She sternly warns those who resist her help.

[21] She crieth in the chief place of concourse, in the openings of the gates: in the city she uttereth her words, saying,

A herald was usually a representative of royalty or a government official, having as his main responsibility the proclamation of an important message (Daniel 3:4). Here the public cry of lady wisdom warns the city dwellers at the most trafficked locations, at the head of the *cardo* (main street) where the smaller streets converge (Ezekiel 16:25) and at the city gate (Ruth 4:1) which was the hub of daily life. The clear and public voice of lady wisdom is contrasted to the secret plots of wicked sinners (1:10).

[22] How long, ye simple ones, will ye love simplicity? and the scorners delight in their scorning, and fools hate knowledge?

Longing for these men to turn from their evil ways and live, the herald or lady wisdom poses three questions to those who pass through the busy city. The rebellious passersby fit into one of three categories.

The "simple," or open-minded, are the recruits of the wicked group; the "scorners," or those who are self-sufficiently proud, are the leaders of their rebel army; and finally, "fools," or stupid people, confident in their own wisdom, are the rank and file.

[23] Turn you at my reproof: behold, I will pour out my spirit unto you, I will make known my words unto you.

Lady wisdom, not willing that any should perish, pleads with the three previously mentioned classes to receive three solutions to their folly. Begin by taking "my reproof"; repentance of evil leads to an over-flowing of "my spirit," causing "my words" or wisdom to abide in them.

[24] Because I have called, and ye refused; I have stretched out my hand, and no man regarded;

In her last appeal, the voice of lady wisdom, which has called so often (though they wouldn't come) and reached out so steadfastly (though they paid no attention), now transitions from an invitation to salvation to a threat of damnation.

[25] But ye have set at nought all my counsel, and would none of my reproof:

Day after day, year after year, they rejected her advice as having no value and were not willing to be inclined to the correction she offered through their parents and the elders. It is one thing to not know one's sins, but it is a fearful thing to know them and willfully choose not to change them!

[26] I also will laugh at your calamity; I will mock when your fear cometh;

Because they did not hearken or obey her voice, when the unwise cry out for help lady wisdom will not hear them; she will even hide her face from them at that time, because they have behaved wickedly in their doings (Micah 3:4). Verses 26-27 predict the outcome for the unwise.

[27] When your fear cometh as desolation, and your destruction cometh as a whirlwind; when distress and anguish cometh upon you

The destructive imagery in this verse is borrowed from nature. Because of their own foolishness, calamity overtakes them like a mighty storm, and disaster engulfs them like a whirlwind. Since they have not hearkened to wisdom's voice, their lives are one series of calamities after another.

[28] Then shall they call upon me, but I will not answer; they shall seek me early, but they shall not find me:

Instead of wisdom crying to the fools, now the fools cry to wisdom. The simple, the scorners, and the fools who did not listen to her voice while it was "near" (Isaiah 55:6) now call upon lady wisdom, who has "risen up, and shut the door" (Luke 13:25). She will not hearken to their cries of desperation.

[29] For that they hated knowledge, and did not choose the fear of the LORD:

Because the fools consistently refused her advice, they now must pay the consequences for rejecting the teacher's basic theme and the motto of the book: the first step toward knowledge is having a reverential fear of YHWH (1:7).

[30] They would none of my counsel: they despised all my reproof.

Here the author recapitulates the reasons why lady wisdom has hidden her face, namely because the fools rejected her advice as having no value and were not willing to be inclined to the correction she offered (1:25).

[31] Therefore shall they eat of the fruit of their own way, and be filled with their own devices.

As a result of their conduct, they must reap what they have sown and eat the bitter fruit of living their own way. That which was sweet at the time it was eaten has now stuffed their stomach with bitterness. Verses 31-32 predict the outcome for the unwise.

[32] For the turning away of the simple shall slay them, and the prosperity of fools shall destroy them.

The simple (or open-minded) turn away from lady wisdom into the arms of death, whereas the wise turn and embrace her and live. Fools are destroyed by their own intellectual and spiritual ease or complacency, whereas the wise man will be wiser still in his pursuit of a higher truth.

[33] But whoso hearkeneth unto me shall dwell safely, and shall be quiet from fear of evil.

Lady wisdom now brings her discourse to a conclusion by contrasting the danger of the foolish with the confidence and security that wisdom provides in times of calamity for those who hearken unto or obey her voice.

Proverbs 2

[1] My son, if thou wilt receive my words, and hide my commandments with thee;

The third discourse of the book, like many others in this book, begins with the heading "my son." It comprises the entirety of chapter 2, which describes the benefits that come from a sincere search for wisdom. The first section of the third discourse is from verses 1 to 8 and details the responsibilities of the young man to find the knowledge of God. The traditions (verbally handed down instruction) of an oral society had the advantage of an undeniable intimacy and directness in parental teaching, which in the case of Israel was ideally in accordance with Scripture. The intimacy with the commandments is somewhat lost when the stories are written down. Putting words down permanently in writing actually places them outside the heart, while the seat of emotion lies inside the heart. A print culture can indeed have a rich and imaginative religious literature, but its dependence on the written word inevitably creates distance between the community and its faith and practice. Avoiding this unfortunate separation, the teacher instructs the son to "hide my commandments with thee" in his heart.

[2] So that thou incline thine ear unto wisdom, and apply thine heart to understanding;

The voice of the teacher here is no longer lady wisdom; it is the father again. The father commands the son to bend the outward vehicle for understanding (his ear) and the inward vehicle (his heart) to understand his father's doctrine.

[3] Yea, if thou criest after knowledge, and liftest up thy voice for understanding;

The father promises the son that if he earnestly persists in his quest for wisdom by crying out for her when he needs her, as she herself cries out for him (1:20), that voice will lead him to knowledge and understanding. These two synonyms for wisdom are from the root meaning "between"; the voice of the teachings of his father and mother will be between his ears and stored up in his heart.

[4] If thou seekest her as silver, and searchest for her as for hid treasures;

The father implores the son to fully commit to the difficulties of seeking after wisdom with the energy and passion he would employ in mining for silver and hidden treasures. Earlier the rewards for finding wisdom were comparable to a golden chain (1:9); here they are equivalent to precious metals. Though the difficulties and commitment of seeking wisdom is the principal matter, the idea is rooted in the culture of the ancients, who were familiar with seeking after the treasures of a deceased man who had not disclosed the exact location of his hidden belongings (Matthew 13:44).

[5] Then shalt thou understand the fear of the LORD, and find the knowledge of God.

If the son employs his efforts not as a casual observer but as a totally dedicated pursuer of wisdom, his reward or discovery will result reciprocally in a reverential fear of YHWH. Thus, he will have found the greatest of all treasures, the knowledge of God.

[6] For the LORD giveth wisdom: out of his mouth cometh knowledge and understanding.

YHWH is the fountainhead of all wisdom. His divine knowledge can be channeled from that holy fountain through the student, who can then employ it in order to move from immaturity to maturity.

[7] He layeth up sound wisdom for the righteous: he is a buckler to them that walk uprightly.

Expanding on the idea that wisdom issues only from YHWH, "sound wisdom" (also translated "abiding success") is here stored up by God for the righteous. The father also teaches the son that God shields his children from that which can harm them.

[8] He keepeth the paths of judgment, and preserveth the way of his saints.

Expanding on the idea of YHWH protecting those who are upright, YHWH promises to guard those who are upright yet vulnerable on the paths of life. Paths in antiquity were often frequented by bandits and robbers who preyed on travelers, thus the spiritual application (Luke 10:30).

[9] Then shalt thou understand righteousness, and judgment, and equity; yea, every good path.

When the son has committed to earnestly seeking after wisdom like a treasure, then he will understand what is right, just, and fair, finding the right way to go in the paths of life. The second section of this discourse is from verses 9-19 and details the results of the wisdom the son has diligently attained.

[10] When wisdom entereth into thine heart, and knowledge is pleasant unto thy soul;

The advantages wisdom gives the son once it is hidden in his heart makes him at perfect peace, even with his enemies, because his heart and soul are fixed on the pleasant commandments of his teacher.

[11] Discretion shall preserve thee, understanding shall keep thee:

Discretion, the outward manifestation of godly wisdom, "preserves" or guides the many choices the son daily makes. Before, God protected the son (2:8); now, his own understanding (flowing from a fear of YHWH) accomplishes this as he progresses from immaturity to maturity.

[12] To deliver thee from the way of the evil man, from the man that speaketh froward things;

The son's wise choices are here promised to watch over him and keep him safe, retaining his honor and pleasing his teacher and his God, as he is delivered from "froward things" or perversions of the truth.

[13] Who leave the paths of uprightness, to walk in the ways of darkness;

These evil men, the son's potential associates, have turned from the straight path of obeying wisdom to habitually walk down crooked paths under the cover of darkness to conceal their wicked ways. In verses 13-15 the teacher gives a more detailed account of the character of those who would attempt to persuade the son to leave the way of righteousness.

[14] Who rejoice to do evil, and delight in the frowardness of the wicked;

The son's contemporaries, as ancient Israelites, knew God's justice required that those who did these things deserve to die, yet they did them anyway. Worse yet, they encouraged others like the teacher's son to do them, thus displaying the worst state of depravity (Romans 1:32).

[15] Whose ways are crooked, and they froward in their paths:

Finishing the theme of paths and the ways of evil men, the teacher warns the son of the "crooked" or twisted and distorted choices of his friends who are "froward," seeking to turn him aside with them.

[16] To deliver thee from the strange woman, even from the stranger which flattereth with her words;

Not only will the wisdom instilled in the son by his teacher save him from immoral men, but also from the immoral woman who would use smooth talk to entangle the son (1:16-19). These "strangers" are not non-Israelites but include divorced Israelite women.

[17] Which forsaketh the guide of her youth, and forgetteth the covenant of her God.

Wisdom protects the young man from the silly woman who has abandoned the husband of her youth, ignoring the wedding vow of faithfulness she made to her husband before God. In ancient Israel women were not permitted to divorce their husbands, therefore a wife's options in a difficult marriage were either to stick it out or to seek pleasure elsewhere.

[18] For her house inclineth unto death, and her paths unto the dead.

Apparently, adultery and divorce had become commonplace in ancient Israel. The teacher warns the son of the deadly consequences of fornication. This immoral, steep path descends through the house of this married, adulterous woman and will lead the son to certain death.

[19] None that go unto her return again, neither take they hold of the paths of life.

The man who engages the strange woman in adultery is doomed, traveling past the point of no return down a one-way road. A return from that world of death and fornication to the paths of life is deemed all but impossible.

[20] That thou mayest walk in the way of good men, and keep the paths of the righteous.

The words of the teacher advise the young man to follow the steps of good men instead and to stay on the paths of the righteous. Verses 20-22 are the conclusion of this discourse and combine words of encouragement on the one hand and warning on the other.

[21] For the upright shall dwell in the land, and the perfect shall remain in it.

The reward of the wise man, who honors his father and his mother by overcoming the temptations presented in this discourse, includes the inheritance and promise "that thy days may be long upon the land which the LORD thy God giveth thee" (Exodus 20:12).

[22] But the wicked shall be cut off from the earth, and the transgressors shall be rooted out of it.

Here the teacher warns the son as he contrasts the fate of the righteous with the wicked. The immoral man or woman will not receive the inheritance of land and family but will be forcibly removed from the land of the living, uprooted and disposed of like an unwanted and dangerous plant.

PROVERBS 3

[1] My son, forget not my law; but let thine heart keep my commandments:

This verse begins the fourth discourse of the book (3:1-10), which continues the two main themes thus far: the requirements of living a wise life and the rewards that come from it. The father implores the son to not forget his *torah*, his instruction or direction, but to hide it in his heart. Apparently, the word *torah* is from a verb meaning "throw" which came to mean distribute and eventually teach. The emphasis on memorization was an anthropological phenomenon among cultures that influenced Jewish thought and practice. In the countries within Israel's sphere of influence, the mind or heart stood at the center of the oral-written crossing point. The focus in these surrounding cultures, as in Israel, was on inscribing their most precious traditions, here the words of the teacher, on the insides of their people (i.e., entrenched in their memories).

[2] For length of days, and long life, and peace, shall they add to thee.

If the son obeys the commandments of his teacher, thus honoring his father, he is promised to live many years (Exodus 20:12) and to have a prosperous life, thus having a harmonious relationship within his family. He is whole or complete (*shalom*) in all aspects of his life.

[3] Let not mercy and truth forsake thee: bind them about thy neck; write them upon the table of thine heart:

The honorable attributes of wise living—*hesed* (faithfulness, loyalty, love, or mercy) and *emet* (similar to our "amen," meaning "accuracy" or "truth")—are to adorn the young man inside and out for all to see.

[4] So shalt thou find favour and good understanding in the sight of God and man.

By obeying the teachings of his father and publicly displaying *hesed* and *emet*, the young man will obtain the highest levels of a complete and prosperous life. He will find favor (grace or amiability) along with prudence (discernment), which together bring success with both God and people.

[5] Trust in the LORD with all thine heart; and lean not unto thine own understanding.

The young man's confidence in the truth of the Word of God to help him attain wisdom is not to be halfhearted but complete and accomplished "with all his heart." This is in stark opposition to the warning against the self-sufficiency of the fool in his quest for wisdom.

[6] In all thy ways acknowledge him, and he shall direct thy paths.

Here we have a cause-and-effect statement. The teacher promises the son is that if he seeks God's will in all he does (the cause) then God will give him wisdom to make the right choices, or God will "direct," literally "make straight," the normally crooked paths of life before him (the effect).

[7] Be not wise in thine own eyes: fear the LORD, and depart from evil.

Approaching the same thought as in the previous two verses but in a different way, the teacher challenges the son to be like Job, who "was perfect and upright, and one that feared God, and eschewed evil" (Job 1:1).

[8] It shall be health to thy navel, and marrow to thy bones.

The moral and physical condition of the young man are connected; the pursuit of wise living makes the center or core of his body healthy, literally watering or refreshing ("marrow") his entire body.

[9] Honour the LORD with thy substance, and with the firstfruits of all thine increase:

In the conclusion of this discourse (3:1-10), the teacher explains from his experience—within the ancient Israelite worldview of cause and effect—the benefits that will come to the son if he honors God with the best of his best.

[10] So shall thy barns be filled with plenty, and thy presses shall burst out with new wine.

The teacher finishes with a promise to the young man as he encourages him to give the cream of the crop of his finances to YHWH's service. The teacher gives a great motive: multiplication of resources, which at first appears selfish but is in reality a reward of the young man's faith.

[11] My son, despise not the chastening of the LORD; neither be weary of his correction:

With the heading "my son," we have the fifth discourse of the book (3:11-20). The father warns the son not to reject YHWH's discipline nor to resent when YHWH corrects him. Perhaps the father also warns the son of potential suffering to counter the previous verses' promises of health and material blessings to those who please God. He doesn't want his son to see God's uncomfortable correction as a bad thing.

[12] For whom the LORD loveth he correcteth; even as a father the son in whom he delighteth.

The physical and spiritual blessings that wisdom would bring to the young man have already been enumerated (3:1-10), but if he has to suffer in his pursuit of wisdom he is not to be discouraged (3:11-12). The young man is warned that the spiritual discipline from God will be as difficult as the physical discipline from his own father.

[13] Happy is the man that findeth wisdom, and the man that getteth understanding.

The young man is not to be disheartened when the path gets difficult in his quest for wisdom, because, as the remainder of this discourse shows, it is worth the cost (3:13-20). Another reward wisdom bestows upon those who diligently seek her—besides long life (3:2), acceptance (3:4), good health (3:8), and prosperity (3:10)—is happiness.

[14] For the merchandise of it is better than the merchandise of silver, and the gain thereof than fine gold.

The profits or dividends gained in dealing with wisdom are greater than that which a young man could earn in trading the best precious metals in the open market. Wisdom makes the young man richer than money ever will.

[15] She is more precious than rubies: and all the things thou canst desire are not to be compared unto her.

Continuing the train of thought, wisdom is also better than "rubies," a descriptive word used to denote precious stones in general. The young man's enthusiasm on his quest for wisdom should exceed the zeal one would employ in acquiring earthly treasures, whether precious metals or precious stones.

[16] Length of days is in her right hand; and in her left hand riches and honour.

Lady wisdom is here portrayed as a wise and gracious woman distributing health and long life (a hallmark of the blessings of God; Psalm 91:16) from her favored hand, the right hand, and distributing wealth of secondary importance out of her inferior hand, the left.

[17] Her ways are ways of pleasantness, and all her paths are peace.

If the young man partakes of that which lady wisdom offers, it is promised that she will guide him, not down a path or life of chaos and folly, but down delightful paths. She will lead the young man to his final destination called peace.

[18] She is a tree of life to them that lay hold upon her: and happy is every one that retaineth her.

Wisdom here becomes equally as life-giving to those who seize and retain her (who enjoy her fruit) as the actual tree of life. Whoever ate of the tree of life would live forever (Genesis 3:22).

[19] The LORD by wisdom hath founded the earth; by understanding hath he established the heavens.

The parental wisdom and advice offered to the son thus far in the book comes from the same divine source and is no different from that cosmic wisdom employed by God Himself when He created.

[20] By his knowledge the depths are broken up, and the clouds drop down the dew.

When the fountains of the great deep erupt and water the earth, and when rain drops fall (a softer method of watering the earth), the wisdom of God is at work. In the conclusion of this discourse, the teacher states that not only did God use wisdom to make the world, He also employs it now to run the earth. This power, divine wisdom, is also available to the son.

[21] My son, let not them depart from thine eyes: keep sound wisdom and discretion:

With the heading "my son," we have the sixth discourse of the book (3:21-35). It is not enough for the son to diligently locate and acquire wisdom; since it is so powerful, he has to retain it by any means necessary.

[22] So shall they be life unto thy soul, and grace to thy neck.

The wisdom the son retains and the correct decisions he thus makes will bless him with long life (an indicator of the favor of God). Too, his "wisdom and discretion" bring him honor publicly, much in the way that a golden necklace would adorn a man of distinction (Genesis 43:42).

[23] Then shalt thou walk in thy way safely, and thy foot shall not stumble.

When the young man finds and retains lady wisdom, she shall have charge over the young man's life to keep and protect him in all his ways. Wisdom will bear him up in her hands lest he "dash his foot" against a stone on the paths of life.

[24] When thou liest down, thou shalt not be afraid: yea, thou shalt lie down, and thy sleep shall be sweet.

The wise lie down in peace and sleep because the Lord alone makes them dwell in safety (Psalm 4:8). Verses 24-26 expand on the theme of the previous verse, assuring the young man of the watch that wisdom keeps over those who value her.

[25] Be not afraid of sudden fear, neither of the desolation of the wicked, when it cometh.

Those who have wisdom as their refuge and fortress have no reason to fear the desolation or storm of the wicked, whether it comes as a terror at night or in the form of an arrow that flies by day (Psalm 91).

[26] For the LORD shall be thy confidence, and shall keep thy foot from being taken.

The reason the wise have no cause to fear is that YHWH Himself is the source of their security. The father promises the son that the wisdom that YHWH disseminates will keep his foot from being caught in a metaphorical trap. Exegetically we must not try to distinguish too carefully between God and His wisdom.

[27] Withhold not good from them to whom it is due, when it is in the power of thine hand to do it.

Here the father teaches the son that when he has opportunity, he should do good to all men (Galatians 6:10). Throughout the rest of this discourse the wise man is known as charitable, peaceful, and content

(3:27-30), not one who imitates or associates with violent men (3:31-35).

[28] Say not unto thy neighbour, Go, and come again, and to morrow I will give; when thou hast it by thee.

Continuing the theme of charity from the previous verse, the son is also to be the model neighbor, loving his neighbor as himself. Therefore, whenever he is in position to do a deed of kindness, he should do so without delay.

[29] Devise not evil against thy neighbour, seeing he dwelleth securely by thee.

The father warns the son to never abuse the confidence his neighbor has in him by plotting harm against his house. Anyone who devises evil against those who live safely nearby, who would naturally trust in the hospitality and benevolence of their friend, abuses the second greatest commandment (Matthew 22:39).

[30] Strive not with a man without cause, if he have done thee no harm.

The wise man is known to live peaceably with all men, never seeking to quarrel with another (Romans 12:18). Yet if the situation arises where another man strives with him without good reason, he is taught by his father to defend himself.

[31] Envy thou not the oppressor, and choose none of his ways.

As the discourse comes to an end, the father warns the son not to be jealous of or even to associate with "the oppressor," or literally "a man of violence." Neither is he to follow the ways or paths the violent man has taken to achieve his temporal success.

[32] For the froward is abomination to the LORD: but his secret is with the righteous.

The froward, or distorters of the truth, are detestable to God. But the wise needn't worry since they are God's friends to whom He imparts wisdom as men do with their friends.

[33] The curse of the LORD is in the house of the wicked: but he blesseth the habitation of the just.

Another motive for the son to seek after wisdom is that YHWH gives people what they deserve. For example, YHWH curses the house, the person, the posterity, and the property of the detestable but blesses the house of the upright.

[34] Surely he scorneth the scorners: but he giveth grace unto the lowly.

YHWH repays scorners, those who talk arrogantly and mock at sin, with scorn. On the other hand, He is gracious to those humble ones who have been afflicted by the mocking and temptations of those scorners.

[35] The wise shall inherit glory: but shame shall be the promotion of fools.

In the world of the Bible, honor was enviable. Honor was paid to worthy men in thought, word, deed, or substance. In fact, ancient laws pronounced the death penalty on those who dishonored parents in act or word (Exodus 21:15). The greatest privilege the wise can inherit is given here, specifically an honorable name, which is contrasted with the most unfortunate fate, being known as a shameful fool.

Proverbs 4

[1] Hear, ye children, the instruction of a father, and attend to know understanding.

With the heading "my son," or "my children" depending on your translation, we have the seventh discourse of the book (4:1-9), which functions as an autobiography of the teacher. The teacher advises his student to be absorbed with his teaching so that he may become intimately involved with discerning what is wise and foolish. Verses 1-4 are an introduction to the teacher's autobiography.

[2] For I give you good doctrine, forsake ye not my law.

The reason the teacher requests the attention of his student is that he is about to give him good guidance, the guidance that his own father had given him years ago. The teacher warns his child not to turn away from his *torah* or instruction to that of someone else.

[3] For I was my father's son, tender and only beloved in the sight of my mother.

The teacher was once in the same position with his father as his favored son now is. The sense is that wisdom is passed down from parents to children; we see the father impressing on his son sound advice. The small pieces found here of autobiographical data from Solomon's early years harmonize with what little we know of him from the historical books (1 Chronicles 29:1).

[4] He taught me also, and said unto me, Let thine heart retain my words: keep my commandments, and live.

From 4:4 to at least 4:9 it appears we have a summary of the wisdom David taught Solomon (1 Chronicles 28:9). David taught his successor to take his words to heart with the promise that if he kept his father's commandments he would live a long and happy life (a hallmark of a life blessed by God).

[5] Get wisdom, get understanding: forget it not; neither decline from the words of my mouth.

After the introduction, the father's instruction here becomes more specific as he provides a sample of his teaching style. He not only advises the son on what to do (attain and retain wisdom) but also on what not to do (don't refuse the source of wisdom).

[6] Forsake her not, and she shall preserve thee: love her, and she shall keep thee.

Perhaps another example of David's teaching style is evident here; short, pithy statements using both negative and positive commands followed by consequences. In response to being obeyed by the son, lady wisdom shall protect and watch over the son in all aspects of his life.

[7] Wisdom is the principal thing; therefore get wisdom: and with all thy getting get understanding.

Speaking from experience, the father teaches the son what his father taught him: the most excellent possession of all is wisdom. Though it might cost everything the young son has, he needs to attain it.

[8] Exalt her, and she shall promote thee: she shall bring thee to honour, when thou dost embrace her.

The sense of the verse is that if the young son does something for wisdom, she will do something for him. The young man's response to lady wisdom is to exalt or diligently search for her and then embrace her like he would his wife.

[9] She shall give to thine head an ornament of grace: a crown of glory shall she deliver to thee.

Again, wisdom is portrayed as a head covering (1:9). Once the son has embraced wisdom, she will publicly honor him as a man of distinction marked with a sign of royalty—a conqueror's garland and a golden crown.

[10] Hear, O my son, and receive my sayings; and the years of thy life shall be many.

With the heading "my son," we have the eighth discourse of the book (4:10-19). If the son honors his father by receiving his teachings, he is promised the reward of a long and good life. The son's life could be cut short if he was consistently disobedient like a glutton or drunkard who deprived the family of honor (Deuteronomy 21:20-21).

[11] I have taught thee in the way of wisdom; I have led thee in right paths.

Here the father recalls the instruction he has given the son in the past. He has taught his son how wisdom is to be attained and has caused him to walk down "right" (literally "straight") paths, meaning morally straight paths.

[12] When thou goest, thy steps shall not be straitened; and when thou runnest, thou shalt not stumble.

The preparation of roadbeds in antiquity was limited to the removal of rocks and the leveling of the surface where necessary (Isaiah 62:10). With that cultural background in mind, it becomes clear that because of his education (via his father), the son will not be hampered nor will he stumble as he walks down the paths of life.

[13] Take fast hold of instruction; let her not go: keep her; for she is thy life.

Here the teacher gives the son three commands with the same motive. The only way for the son to ensure that he has a long and blessed life is to "take hold," "not let go," and "keep" what his father has taught him.

[14] Enter not into the path of the wicked, and go not in the way of evil men.

The teacher momentarily changes from instructing to warning his son. The basic theme of the preceding verses is stated again. The young man has the choice of two diametrically opposed paths to walk down, the path of the just or the path of the wicked (1:16).

[15] Avoid it, pass not by it, turn from it, and pass away.

The father warns the son to not only turn away from the temptations posed by wicked men but to "pass away." The sense is to put the greatest possible distance between himself and those who would corrupt his good morals.

[16] For they sleep not, except they have done mischief; and their sleep is taken away, unless they cause some to fall.

The contemporaries of the son have sin as their second nature; they are not able to live without committing premeditated evil. They won't even sleep until they've caused someone to morally stumble. As the son imitates his father, so the wicked imitate their father the devil, both of whom take delight in sin and in the ruin of others (John 8:44).

[17] For they eat the bread of wickedness, and drink the wine of violence.

The dangers surrounding the wise son are numerous; many of his fellows eat, drink, and sleep evil. These wicked men either literally get their sustenance through immoral means, or, figuratively, violence is as necessary to them as food and drink.

[18] But the path of the just is as the shining light, that shineth more and more unto the perfect day.

The next two verses continue the theme of the two contrasting paths for the righteous and the wicked. The path of the young man is portrayed as being lit by the sunrise, an image of salvation for the righteous and judgment on the wicked (Genesis 19:23). This imagery was also used by David in his last speech (2 Samuel 23:4). The way of the wise, like the sun, goes on and on, increasing in brightness as time advances, until at last it reaches its glorious setting for all to see.

[19] The way of the wicked is as darkness: they know not at what they stumble.

In contrast to the bright sun of righteousness, which allows the son to go forth and tread the path of the just safely, is the path of the wicked. Their path is steeped and surrounded in the realm of darkness, causing a man to lose his way and his life.

[20] My son, attend to my words; incline thine ear unto my sayings.

With the heading "my son," we have the ninth discourse of the book (4:20-27). The father continues his teaching after citing the example of his own upbringing and what he learned from that education. That same wisdom is now being orally transmitted to his son and therefore requires that he incline or perk up his ear.

[21] Let them not depart from thine eyes; keep them in the midst of thine heart.

The struggle for winning over the mind of the young man took place in the home. If these teachings were retained in his inward (heart) and outward (eyes) vehicles for learning, he would honor his family with wise living.

[22] For they are life unto those that find them, and health to all their flesh.

The message of the book thus far has emphasized the same conclusion. The leading slogan or ancient philosophy has been illustrated in many ways and from several angles, as in this verse. But in the end, we return to the assertion of the same formula: "The fear of the LORD is the beginning of knowledge" (1:7).

[23] Keep thy heart with all diligence; for out of it are the issues of life.

A study of the Scriptures indicates that the heart, when considered figuratively, is the inner control center of the person. It is the location of human character (Luke 6:45) and is the aspect of the young man about which his father and God are most concerned (1 Samuel 16:7). The heart to the ancient Israelites served as the seat of all the spiritual, moral, intellectual, volitional, and emotional aspects of man's life. The sense of the verse is that the son is to guard his heart above all else since it determines the course of his life.

[24] Put away from thee a froward mouth, and perverse lips put far from thee.

The son is also to avoid "a froward mouth," or literally distortion, the twisting of the truth, and perverse lips that turn aside from the truth, since "a good man out of the good treasure of the heart brings forth good things" (Matthew 12:35).

[25] Let thine eyes look right on, and let thine eyelids look straight before thee.

Wandering eyes can distract the son from focusing on the route and the goal of the book: obeying the teachings of his father to attain the fear of the Lord, which is the beginning of knowledge. The goal is successful living and the route is straight ahead, the way of wisdom.

[26] Ponder the path of thy feet, and let all thy ways be established.

The sense of the verse is that the son is to make straight or level the moral path of his life by removing any obstacle at any cost that would prevent him from living a long and good life (Matthew 5:29).

[27] Turn not to the right hand nor to the left: remove thy foot from evil.

As it would be injurious in the world of the Bible to turn aside from the main path, especially in the night, so the son is warned not to veer off the course his father has set him on but to have unswerving obedience.

PROVERBS 5

[1] My son, attend unto my wisdom, and bow thine ear to my understanding:

With the heading "my son," we have the tenth discourse of the book (5:1-23). Sexual immorality in ancient Israel must have been rampant since the teacher dedicates chapters 5–7 to the theme with only one diversion from the subject (6:1-19). So, the father instructs the son to pay attention and listen carefully to his wise counsel concerning adultery and marriage.

[2] That thou mayest regard discretion, and that thy lips may keep knowledge.

Another possible reason for this warning might have been Solomon's own struggles with this vice, a warning from personal experience. The father's aim is that the son will safeguard this teaching and show discernment when it comes to interacting with women, unlike himself.

[3] For the lips of a strange woman drop as an honeycomb, and her mouth is smoother than oil:

Here the teacher begins the subject of his discourse. The son is warned that the speech of a harlot is tempting and sweet, comparable to honey. The only sweet foodstuffs known in the world of the Bible were natural sugars. Sweet pastes were produced from fruits like dates or grapes or the honey produced by bees. The harlot's speech is also soothing and is compared figuratively to healing oil. Oil was a common remedy for wounds (Isaiah 1:6); the sick were anointed with it (James 5:14). Sometimes wine was added to oil and administered to a wound (Luke 10:34).

[4] But her end is bitter as wormwood, sharp as a two-edged sword.

The father warns the son that although the harlot's enticements may indeed taste as sweet as honey at first, they will invariably end in death, leaving a noxious and poisonous taste in his mouth. What may begin as soothing and healing words to his heart will soon turn to a violent source of remorse.

[5] Her feet go down to death; her steps take hold on hell.

Finishing the brief description and warning concerning the seductress (5:1-5), the teacher summarizes her lifestyle as leading straight to the grave. But if that wasn't enough, the teacher continues, saying that her fate is eternal punishment and torment in hell.

[6] Lest thou shouldest ponder the path of life, her ways are moveable, that thou canst not know them.

In verses 6-14 the father warns the son of the price he must pay for unchastity. To fulfill her own lusts and to prevent the son from choosing the path of life, the harlot will lead the son down dark and devious paths. He will end up as lost as she is.

[7] Hear me now therefore, O ye children, and depart not from the words of my mouth.

In a structure that is typical to the book, the teacher gives a positive command for his sons to listen to him and then follows with a prohibition, imploring them to never stray from what he is about to say. The subject matter is literally a matter of life and death.

[8] Remove thy way far from her, and come not nigh the door of her house:

The father teaches his sons that the greatest protection from such temptations is flight, to flee youthful lusts. The sons are to shun the place where the loose woman dwells. If a lustful look leads to sin, then avoid it at all costs; treat her house as some infectious and contagious deadly disease.

[9] Lest thou give thine honour unto others, and thy years unto the cruel:

If the son disobeys the father and goes in to the harlot, he will lose his honor and forfeit all he has achieved in the best years of his life to "the cruel," the consequences of an avenger without mercy.

[10] Lest strangers be filled with thy wealth; and thy labours be in the house of a stranger;

Another consequence of going in to the harlot is not only the loss of respect and possible disease or death, but also financial ruin as the young man transfers his accumulated wealth to strangers to feed his deadly addiction.

[11] And thou mourn at the last, when thy flesh and thy body are consumed,

After the loss of his honor and his wealth, and being at the end of his rope, the young man's remaining possession, his body, will be totally consumed with the deadly diseases associated with sexual immorality.

[12] And say, How have I hated instruction, and my heart despised reproof;

Reduced to poverty, disgrace, and disease with no one or nothing left to live for, the fool will cry aloud and confess the error of his ways. The momentary pleasure of sin later yields a sure reproach.

[13] And have not obeyed the voice of my teachers, nor inclined mine ear to them that instructed me!

This verse documents the last stage of misery of the foolish young man: regret. If he could only go back in time and listen to the loving instruction of his parents who taught him to avoid sexual immorality, but alas he cannot. He made his bed, and now he must lie in it.

[14] I was almost in all evil in the midst of the congregation and assembly.

Now that the son has come to utter ruin and disgraced the honor of his family, he must face public disgrace and quite possibly execution. In ancient Israel, guilty persons were shamed or worse in a public assembly as a result of their great sin (Deuteronomy 21:20-21).

[15] Drink waters out of thine own cistern, and running waters out of thine own well.

In verses 15-23 the father describes the better path: fidelity. Using a series of metaphors, the father admonishes the son to be faithful to his own wife. Cisterns are artificial reservoirs usually cut into bedrock for collecting and conserving rain runoff. Wells are listed with other costly items (Deuteronomy 6:11), and the ownership of wells was so important that feuds over them were settled at times only by a unique covenant (Genesis 21:25). So, the value of cisterns and wells for survival is comparable to that of a holy marriage.

[16] Let thy fountains be dispersed abroad, and rivers of waters in the streets.

Considering the preciousness of water in the world of the Bible, only a fool would waste his water by throwing it into the street. This idiotic act is parallel to a foolish man disseminating his seed all over town.

[17] Let them be only thine own, and not strangers' with thee.

The children a man brings into this world should be the enjoyment of him and his wife, but immoral intercourse throws major doubt upon the fatherhood of a child. The child may be his, but since he is in company with a whore, it may belong to a stranger.

[18] Let thy fountain be blessed: and rejoice with the wife of thy youth.

The father encourages the son that the blessing of a wise life is that his "fountain" (wife) bears numerous children. The husband is to seek sexual joy not with the harlot but with his wife; the marital bed is the sphere within which he is to find all pleasure.

[19] Let her be as the loving hind and pleasant roe; let her breasts satisfy thee at all times; and be thou ravished always with her love.

The teacher now compares the young man's wife to the most beautiful and graceful of wild animals. The beauty, grace, and physical stature of this woman should satisfy or intoxicate him, giving the young man no reason to look for love anywhere else.

[20] And why wilt thou, my son, be ravished with a strange woman, and embrace the bosom of a stranger?

The father asks the son two rhetorical questions centered around why he would risk destroying his honor, finances, health, and even his very life for those sexual pleasures which he can enjoy daily without sin.

[21] For the ways of man are before the eyes of the LORD, and he pondereth all his goings.

Another reason for showing fidelity to his wife is the reminder that God is omnipresent and omniscient. The tracks or habits the young man makes by constant use are considered under the gaze or scrutiny of God's watchful eye.

[22] His own iniquities shall take the wicked himself, and he shall be holden with the cords of his sins.

The father concludes the discourse with a strong expression of individualism. The fool has sinned so long that he is metaphorically bound hand and foot with the chains of his own terrible decisions.

[23] He shall die without instruction; and in the greatness of his folly he shall go astray.

Here is the fearful end of the adulterer; he will die because of lack of self-control. In an awful climax and through his own folly, he "goes astray" or literally staggers drunkenly to a pathetic end. The son, through his own choices, is the ultimate winner or loser.

PROVERBS 6

[1] My son, if thou be surety for thy friend, if thou hast stricken thy hand with a stranger,

With the heading "my son," we have the eleventh discourse of the book (6:1-19) and a diversion from the subject of sexual immorality to some advice on what pitfalls the young man should avoid. Again, the teacher uses normal daily life settings as the backdrop for helping the son move from immaturity to maturity. The first subject the father warns the son of is foolish business dealings (verses 1-5).

[2] Thou art snared with the words of thy mouth, thou art taken with the words of thy mouth.

Here and in the previous verse the son is warned that if he puts up security for a friend's debt or agrees to guarantee the debt of a stranger, the inevitable consequence will be him being legally trapped in that bad deal.

[3] Do this now, my son, deliver thyself, when thou art come into the hand of thy friend; go, humble thyself, and make sure thy friend.

The father pleads with the son, if he should fall into the trap of placing his freedom and his property at his friend's mercy, that he should swallow his pride and go and beg the creditor to have his name removed from the contract.

[4] Give not sleep to thine eyes, nor slumber to thine eyelids.

Verses 4-5 stress the urgency of acquitting oneself of foolish financial obligations. The father warns the son to not put off prostrating before the creditor. Dealing with tasks promptly is the opposite mindset of many in the land of the Bible (to this very day) who hold to the mantra "it can wait till tomorrow."

[5] Deliver thyself as a roe from the hand of the hunter, and as a bird from the hand of the fowler.

The teacher uses metaphors from nature to highlight the life-or-death scenarios which foolish business dealings can get the young man into. The teacher encourages him to struggle in order to get free from such an ensnarement. The situation could be so dire that the young man might have to sell himself to the creditor as a slave to pay back what he cosigned for.

[6] Go to the ant, thou sluggard; consider her ways, and be wise:

The next pitfall the father warns the son against is laziness (6:6-11). Ants are only mentioned in the Bible here (6:6-8) and in 30:25. The father asks the son to take a lesson from the ants regarding their work ethic. The son is to attend to how hard they work, how heavy their loads are, and how they always seem to be active.

[7] Which having no guide, overseer, or ruler,

Furthermore, since ants are totally independent creatures having no judge, overseer, or king to make them work all day every day, they should be commended and mimicked even all the more for their initiative and work ethic.

[8] Provideth her meat in the summer, and gathereth her food in the harvest.

Finally, the diligent ants have the foresight to plan ahead as they gather food during the hot summer so they can survive the harsh winter; this business principle the young man is encouraged to emulate.

[9] How long wilt thou sleep, O sluggard? when wilt thou arise out of thy sleep?

Totally out of patience with his slothful student, the teacher twice asks the sluggard when he is going to grow up and take responsibility for his own life. Verses 9-11 are a call to the sluggard to awake from his stupor and a warning of the dire consequences he will face if he remains lazy.

[10] Yet a little sleep, a little slumber, a little folding of the hands to sleep:

Here the father quotes the young man's response as he attempts to awake him from bed saying "just a little extra sleep, then I will get up." The young son is warned that habits of laziness and indulgence can quickly grow on the best of people.

[11] So shall thy poverty come as one that travelleth, and thy want as an armed man.

The sluggard's repeated actions and habits necessitate life and death consequences. The young man finds himself financially destroyed because of his own laziness, but a robber didn't steal all his money; his own sleep did.

[12] A naughty person, a wicked man, walketh with a froward mouth.

The next series of pitfalls the father warns the son against are deceit and malice (6:12-19). The word for a "naughty" person is literally belial; eventually belial became explicitly a name for the devil, who is the father of all such evil qualities (2 Corinthians 6:15).

[13] He winketh with his eyes, he speaketh with his feet, he teacheth with his fingers;

Feet and fingers are frequently used in the East as a means of secretly communicating deceitful ideas in the presence of those from whom it is intended to conceal the information. These deceivers are the type of people the young man is to stay away from. "Whoever has shifty eyes plots mischief and those who know him will keep their distance. In your presence he uses honeyed talk, and admires your words, but later he changes his tone and twists the words to your ruin" (Sirach 27:22-23).

[14] Frowardness is in his heart, he deviseth mischief continually; he soweth discord.

Behind the external mask of gestures and facial expressions is an inward man to avoid and despise. "I have hated many things, but not as much as him, and the LORD hates him as well" (Sirach 27:24). Such deceivers have perverted hearts that plot evil and are constantly stirring up trouble to advance their own purpose.

[15] Therefore shall his calamity come suddenly; suddenly shall he be broken without remedy.

The great sins of the fool have even greater punishments. Here is the fateful end of the deceiver: he will be destroyed suddenly, broken in an instant like a potter's vessel (Psalm 2:9), beyond all hope of healing.

[16] These six things doth the LORD hate: yea, seven are an abomination unto him:

Verses 16-19 more specifically describe and complete the character traits of the previously mentioned man of belial, seven detestable attitudes, thoughts, words, actions, and influences that YHWH hates.

[17] A proud look, a lying tongue, and hands that shed innocent blood,

The list covers the wicked man's evil character from head to toe. The enumeration begins with the lofty eyes then moves downward to the lying tongue and further still to the murderous disposition of the wicked man.

[18] An heart that deviseth wicked imaginations, feet that be swift in running to mischief,

The list of misused body parts continues with the inner control center (heart) and finally gets down to the swift feet, showing the eagerness with which wicked men go to fulfill their lusts. A wicked heart shows that the entire being of the man has turned; his perverted heart plots evil.

[19] A false witness that speaketh lies, and he that soweth discord among brethren.

The teacher lists two more of the seven deadly sins YHWH hates, namely bearing false witness against your neighbor (Exodus 20:16) and—saving the worst for last—the sin of driving wedges between friends, neighbors, and relatives.

[20] My son, keep thy father's commandment, and forsake not the law of thy mother:

With the heading "my son," we have the twelfth discourse of the book (6:20-35) and a return to the subject of sexual immorality which started in 5:1. The father hopes that his son will obey his parents' commandments, unlike Esau, who took a strange wife which was "a grief of mind unto Isaac and Rebekah" (Genesis 26:34-35).

[21] Bind them continually upon thine heart, and tie them about thy neck.

The main moral concern of the father was the spiritual condition of the son's heart. A well-stocked and active mind, full of memorized instruction, was held to be the mother of virtue. What is in a person's heart inevitably showed up in their actions. For an archaeological example of the Torah bound about the neck in the form of an amulet, see the "Silver Scrolls" (Spring 2005, *Bible and Spade*).

[22] When thou goest, it shall lead thee; when thou sleepest, it shall keep thee; and when thou awakest, it shall talk with thee.

Virtue and memorization of the Torah were inextricably linked in the Jewish mind. The ancient Israelites associated intelligence with memorization of, retention of, and obedience to Torah. The Bible, as in these verses, frequently has admonitions to recite God's instructions lest they be forgotten. "Recite these instructions when you stay at home and when you are away, when you lie down and when you get up" (Deuteronomy 6:7).

[23] For the commandment is a lamp; and the law is light; and reproofs of instruction are the way of life:

Almost every key word in the book of Proverbs is included in this verse: commandment, lamp, law, light, reproof, instruction, way, and life. The repetition of key words throughout a work provides the listener or reader with a thread of continuity which will serve to bind the train of thought together in the process of memorization. This technique of repetition is characteristic of the oral culture; in Hebrew literature it was developed into a creative literary device. This handy mnemonic helps the young man remember the teachings of his father since it puts stress on the prominent key words.

[24] To keep thee from the evil woman, from the flattery of the tongue of a strange woman.

Spoken words in ancient Israel as well as neighboring regions were not merely means of communication but objects of power. If the son can memorize and implement his parents' instruction, it will keep him from the immoral woman.

[25] Lust not after her beauty in thine heart; neither let her take thee with her eyelids.

Lady wisdom does not want to lose the young man to another woman, the immoral woman. Thus she warns him of the eyes of the wayward woman, which have perhaps been adorned with eyeliner in an attempt to beautify and enlarge them so as to arrest his gaze (2 Kings 9:30).

[26] For by means of a whorish woman a man is brought to a piece of bread: and the adulteress will hunt for the precious life.

The sense of the verse is that the price of a one-night stand with a prostitute is only the price of a loaf of bread, but the price of sleeping with another man's wife will cost the young man his life at the hands of her husband.

[27] Can a man take fire in his bosom, and his clothes not be burned?

This and the following verse ask rhetorical questions to demonstrate the destruction that illicit sexual relations can have. The illustration is quite obvious: if you play with fire, you are likely to get burned.

[28] Can one go upon hot coals, and his feet not be burned?

The fire metaphors show how obviously dangerous sexual immorality is. Taking a strange woman to his bosom and against his feet (perhaps a euphemism for the male sex organ) should be as terrifying as embracing and being intimate with coals of fire.

[29] So he that goeth in to his neighbour's wife; whosoever toucheth her shall not be innocent.

This verse is the application of the illustrations. Whoever lies with the adulteress or touches her in a carnal way shall be punished as a criminal either by her husband or perhaps by the government in the form of capital punishment for breaking the Torah (Leviticus 20:10).

[30] Men do not despise a thief, if he steal to satisfy his soul when he is hungry;

People in ancient Israel were taught not to steal (Exodus 20:15), and they did despise a thief regardless of their excuse or motivation; if somebody who only stole food was an object of contempt by the people, how much more someone who steals another man's wife!

[31] But if he be found, he shall restore sevenfold; he shall give all the substance of his house.

According to the Torah the guilty party had to reimburse the offended party up to five times what was stolen (Exodus 22:1). Probably using seven as a poetic number, the teacher says that if the bread thief is caught, he must pay back seven times what he stole, even if he has to sell everything in his house.

[32] But whoso committeth adultery with a woman lacketh understanding: he that doeth it destroyeth his own soul.

But the adulterer has to pay for his sin with his life. Like adultery, a few coals of fire can momentarily warm your lap and some hot coals can warm your feet on a cold night, but they can also destroy you.

[33] A wound and dishonour shall he get; and his reproach shall not be wiped away.

The fate or lot of the adulterer is physical punishment at the hands of the offended husband and public disgrace. The shame of the adulterer's sexual immorality will never be erased in his tight-knit, conservative, slow-paced, ancient community. This shame will last for generations.

[34] For jealousy is the rage of a man: therefore he will not spare in the day of vengeance.

The woman's jealous husband will obviously be furious and show no mercy when he takes vengeance, executing both the adulterer and the adulteress, thus putting away evil from Israel (Deuteronomy 22:22).

[35] He will not regard any ransom; neither will he rest content, though thou givest many gifts.

Bribery might work in some situations, but no restitution will suffice for the offended husband. No deal for the life of the adulterer and adulteress can be made; the husband's demands are biblical and non-negotiable: death for both under the dispensation of the Law of Moses (Leviticus 20:10).

PROVERBS 7

[1] My son, keep my words, and lay up my commandments with thee.

With the heading "my son," we have the thirteenth discourse of the book (7:1-27) and a continuation of the subject of sexual immorality which started in 5:1. But first there is a brief prologue regarding the importance of keeping the teachings of one's parents (7:1-4). These home-school teachings are based on the Law of Moses but are not necessarily identical to it.

[2] Keep my commandments, and live; and my law as the apple of thine eye.

The life-and-death reality involved in keeping the commandments of his parents requires the young man to keep their instruction as close to him as possible. "The apple of his eye" is an English idiom that catches the meaning of the Hebrew, which literally means "little man." The sense is that when you are as close to someone as possible and staring into their eyes, you see a reflection of yourself, your "little man," in their pupils. In like manner, the son needs to keep his eyes so closely fixed on his father's teachings that they are constantly reflected in his eyes.

[3] Bind them upon thy fingers, write them upon the table of thine heart.

Many instructions in Proverbs focus on a process that has prominent oral and memorization characteristics, like inclining the ear, hearing the words, and applying the heart to the sayings, to name just a few. The student of Proverbs is to memorize the teacher's exact words, to "keep them within your belly," and then perform them orally, "establish the words on your lips." The tablet of the student's heart was the key focus in the teaching texts of Proverbs. A hearing heart or an open ear was the medium by which the heart received, memorized, and obeyed oral instruction.

[4] Say unto wisdom, Thou art my sister; and call understanding thy kinswoman:

The son is commanded to love lady wisdom like he would his own 'achowth, a feminine noun which can mean sister, relative, or bride. Also, he is to make insight as dear to him as his beloved relative. The sense is that lady wisdom is eligible and worthy to be married, unlike the forthcoming adulteress.

[5] That they may keep thee from the strange woman, from the stranger which flattereth with her words.

The father's hope is that the teachings written on the tablet of the young man's heart will come to mind and he will listen to them rather than the flattery of the adulteress. In this way, they will protect him from destroying his own soul.

[6] For at the window of my house I looked through my casement,

Verses 6-27 are a drama, an extended description which shows what happens to young persons who are void of understanding. The scene unfolds through the narration of an unidentified person who describes what he saw from his window (Judges 5:28).

[7] And beheld among the simple ones, I discerned among the youths, a young man void of understanding,

The narrator, looking down upon the busy street below, admits that many of the young men who walked below were "simple ones" or open-minded, easily persuaded or enticed, but only one really stood out through his actions as lacking understanding.

[8] Passing through the street near her corner; and he went the way to her house,

The simple one did not take the main route but snuck around corners, from where he could watch the woman's house without being seen by others. Then the simple one "went the way" (a word used for a slow-stepped procession) toward the house of the adulteress to satisfy his curiosity.

[9] In the twilight, in the evening, in the black and dark night:

Total darkness is now the backdrop of the next scene, as the author uses five different Hebrew words to emphasize that the act took place in the dead of night, out of the sight of anyone the simple one might know.

[10] And, behold, there met him a woman with the attire of an harlot, and subtil of heart.

The young man's watch was rewarded as the strange woman came out to work the street. Never in the world of the Bible would it be permitted for a lady to be alone in public. So, she meets him in the street, dressed in the recognizable outfit of a prostitute (Revelation 17:4). Her face would have been covered with a veil (Genesis 38:14). Perhaps this veil is an indication that the woman keeps her own heart while she steals the simple one's, or maybe the veil hides her true feelings—perhaps of self-loathing—while she sells her body repeatedly.

[11] (She is loud and stubborn; her feet abide not in her house:

This adulterous wife of some poor Israelite is characterized as being brash, stubborn, and never content to stay at home. Her wandering feet contributed to the destruction of the fabric of her society; she did not follow the biblical model of being "discreet, chaste, a keeper of home, good, obedient to her own husband, so that the word of God is not blasphemed" (Titus 2:5).

[12] Now is she without, now in the streets, and lieth in wait at every corner.)

The immoral woman, like lady wisdom, was visible to all. Both made themselves known to the locals in the streets and in the markets, soliciting those passing by with two different cries, one to life and the other to death.

[13] So she caught him, and kissed him, and with an impudent face said unto him,

The verb in the previous verse, "lieth in wait," has the idea of an ambush or attacking by surprise. So now the adulteress has her prey, the simple one, in her net, and not giving him time to reflect immediately arouses him by kissing him.

[14] I have peace offerings with me; this day have I payed my vows.

So, she put on an "impudent face" or hardened her face with a whore's shameless front (Jeremiah 3:3) to declare that she has just made her required peace offerings in the Temple to mark the end of her period (Leviticus 15:19-30); the simple one need not worry about becoming ceremonially unclean or getting her pregnant. And perhaps since the harlot used the technical word "peace offerings" (which had to be eaten on the same day they are offered; Leviticus 7:15), she was inviting him to a feast of food and sex.

[15] Therefore came I forth to meet thee, diligently to seek thy face, and I have found thee.

So, in this calculated effort to persuade the simple one to hire her services, she uses religion to sweeten the pot by stating that the young man was just the one she was waiting for to share this holy meal.

[16] I have decked my bed with coverings of tapestry, with carved works, with fine linen of Egypt.

The whore continues to persuade the young man that everything is prepared for their exotic escapade. Her reclining couch is already spread with beautiful blankets, in fact with the softest and finest striped colored sheets of Egyptian linen.

[17] I have perfumed my bed with myrrh, aloes, and cinnamon.

One can perceive the eye toward detail and the sense of authority which the narrator has as an eyewitness to the above-mentioned event. Perhaps the aged Solomon is using his own foolish past experiences and vice for women as the storyline for this drama.

[18] Come, let us take our fill of love until the morning: let us solace ourselves with loves.

Continuing to persuade the young man to leave the public street and enter her chambers, the woman propositions the simple one that they should not only get drunk but be intoxicated with forbidden love all night long.

[19] For the goodman is not at home, he is gone a long journey:

The two-timing wife, cheating compulsively on her husband to fulfill her sordid lusts, attempts to ease the young man's mind concerning the retaliation of her husband (6:35) by saying that he is on a long-distance business trip and will never find out.

[20] He hath taken a bag of money with him, and will come home at the day appointed.

The woman continues to comfort the nervous adulterer by doubling down on the fact that there is no possible way her husband would come home that night since he took a large sum to cover his expenses and is set to come home in two weeks, on the new moon.

[21] With her much fair speech she caused him to yield, with the flattering of her lips she forced him.

The time for speaking on the street corner is done as she finally persuades the simple one with her speech that his safety is not in danger. Against his conscience, he has been seduced into bed.

[22] He goeth after her straightway, as an ox goeth to the slaughter, or as a fool to the correction of the stocks;

Using animal metaphors depicting the adulteress as out for the kill, the teacher shows that the open-minded fool does not realize the precarious consequences of his decisions any more than a stupid animal sent to the slaughter house. In similar manner, the second metaphor, according to the LXX (Septuagint), depicts the fool as following the woman like a chained dog.

[23] Till a dart strike through his liver; as a bird hasteth to the snare, and knoweth not that it is for his life.

The liver or heart of the young man (4 Qumran, Barki Napshi), the repository of the commandments of his parents, has been destroyed by the female hunter. The young man was like an easily tempted and irrational bird flying straight into the trap of the adulteress. The drama thus ends with the death of the foolish young man.

[24] Hearken unto me now therefore, O ye children, and attend to the words of my mouth.

With the drama now finished, the father demands that his son (singular in the LXX, as in 7:1) listen and pay attention to the application of the drama, the main point, or the moral of the story given in verses 25-27.

[25] Let not thine heart decline to her ways, go not astray in her paths.

The father warns the son to flee youthful lusts and to not go anywhere near immoral women. This will greatly reduce the chances of having his heart stray away toward her; it will help him to keep his feet from wandering down her wayward path to death.

[26] For she hath cast down many wounded: yea, many strong men have been slain by her.

The house of the adulteress is comparable to a battlefield, and she is as effective and mighty as a powerful army whose total number of slain victims reaches a body count similar to the size of an army.

[27] Her house is the way to hell, going down to the chambers of death.

Not only is her house analogous to a battlefield scattered with the carcasses of her victims, but the souls of her victims don't have far to go as her house is also the gateway to hell. Her bedroom is the den of death, and all who travel that path will never return as they take a shortcut to the lowest parts of hell.

PROVERBS 8

[1] Doth not wisdom cry? and understanding put forth her voice?

Though we don't have the typical heading of "my son," chapter 8 is the fourteenth discourse of the first book. The entirety of this discourse is a praise song of wisdom to tell us again how vital she is and where to locate her. Like in 1:20, wisdom is portrayed as a herald. A herald was usually a representative of royalty or a government official, having as their main responsibility the proclamation of an important message (Daniel 3:4). Verses 1-3 are the introduction of that message.

[2] She standeth in the top of high places, by the way in the places of the paths.

In this instance wisdom, which cannot be separated from God because it is part of Him, speaks on His behalf. The presence and influence of lady wisdom, as with the adulterous woman, happens where people converge, at the most trafficked locations, at the head of the *cardo* (main street) where the smaller paths meet (Ezekiel 16:25).

[3] She crieth at the gates, at the entry of the city, at the coming in at the doors.

The public cry or voice of lady wisdom in this chapter tells of her excellence, origin, and benefits. The clear and visible cry of lady wisdom in the gate, the hub of the city, is contrasted to the secret and wicked plots of the adulteress in the previous discourse. The wisdom of God is as relevant in the shopping center (8:1-3) as in heaven itself (8:22).

[4] Unto you, O men, I call; and my voice is to the sons of man.

Here lady wisdom begins to speak by perhaps calling different classes of men, the higher ("men") and the lower ("sons of man") of society to hear her message. In verses 4-11 wisdom is portrayed as a guide for all men and gives reasons for trusting in her.

[5] O ye simple, understand wisdom: and, ye fools, be ye of an understanding heart.

Lady wisdom speaks to those in the busy city center as she longs that they turn from their evil ways and live (1:22). They are called simple or open-minded, the easily deceived, and are the recruits of the fools who are confident in their own wisdom.

[6] Hear; for I will speak of excellent things; and the opening of my lips shall be right things.

Lady wisdom invites those passing by to listen to the important things she is about to say because everything she says is excellent or worthy. The word for "worthy" is related to the word "before" or "in front of," possibly meaning her words are clear and have no hidden meaning. And in like manner everything else she says is "right" or straight; there's no hidden meanings around crooked corners.

[7] For my mouth shall speak truth; and wickedness is an abomination to my lips.

The lady wisdom now, rather than the father, makes the appeal to do what is right as she, like the teacher, speaks only truth and detests every kind of deception. Almost every verse includes lady wisdom using the pronouns "I," "my," or "me."

[8] All the words of my mouth are in righteousness; there is nothing froward or perverse in them.

The tale of two women continues. The words of lady adulteress are deceptive and tempting, comparable to honey and healing oil (5:3). On the contrary, the words of lady wisdom are straight and can be trusted as not being "froward" or crooked.

[9] They are all plain to him that understandeth, and right to them that find knowledge.

As lady wisdom continues to give reasons for men to trust in her (8:4-11), she states that her words are easy to be understood. Her speech is like a hidden treasure; the man who searches them out will be greatly rewarded.

[10] Receive my instruction, and not silver; and knowledge rather than choice gold.

Lady wisdom pleads with men walking in the marketplace to fully forsake the efforts of gaining the whole world apart from wisdom. Instead, they should seek that which cannot be bought and is eternal, divine wisdom.

[11] For wisdom is better than rubies; and all the things that may be desired are not to be compared to it.

Continuing the train of thought, wisdom is also better than "rubies," a descriptive word used to denote precious stones in general. The young man's enthusiasm on his quest for wisdom should exceed the zeal one would employ in acquiring earthly treasures, whether precious metals or precious stones.

[12] I wisdom dwell with prudence, and find out knowledge of witty inventions.

As man is indwelt by his spirit, so wisdom inhabits or has taken up residence with its counterpart prudence. Prudence is shrewdness or cunning awareness which helps men to attain "right counsels" and signifies that wisdom presides over all of man's well-thought-out plans. In verses 12-21, the heart of the discourse, wisdom displays her superior excellence.

[13] The fear of the LORD is to hate evil: pride, and arrogancy, and the evil way, and the froward mouth, do I hate.

We have already been told in the motto or philosophy of the book that the beginning of wisdom is the fear of YHWH (1:7), but here we are told what wisdom is not. It is not evil, pride, arrogance, corruption, and perverse speech. Because there can never be any harmony between wisdom and folly, if we love the one we must hate the other.

[14] Counsel is mine, and sound wisdom: I am understanding; I have strength.

Having declared what wisdom hates and is not in the previous verse, wisdom now states what she is and what she can bestow on her followers. Wisdom as God's representative has the necessary resources to help man achieve God's will.

[15] By me kings reign, and princes decree justice.

If lady wisdom is needed for the common man to evade fellowshipping with thieves, avoiding the adulteress, and refraining from bad business deals, how much more is she needed by rulers to rule their kingdoms wisely!

[16] By me princes rule, and nobles, even all the judges of the earth.

All classes of royal society and government rule well because they are wise. In the ancient Near East (ANE), judgment of difficult cases was an essential part of a king's responsibilities; take for example the account of the judgment of Solomon (1 Kings 3:16-28).

[17] I love them that love me; and those that seek me early shall find me.

The idea that those who love wisdom are regarded in favor by God is a familiar theme in wisdom literature: "And them that love her [wisdom] the LORD doth love" (Sirach 4:14) and "for God loves nothing so much as the man who lives with wisdom" (Wisdom of Solomon 7:28). The promise that "those who seek [her] early [or better, earnestly] shall find her" is another theme repeated in wisdom literature: "And they that seek her [wisdom] shall be filled with joy" (Sirach 4:12).

[18] Riches and honour are with me; yea, durable riches and righteousness.

In continuing to display her superior excellence (8:12-21), wisdom declares that those who possess her also have access to enduring wealth and prosperity in the form of an endowment of wise counsel from which to draw.

[19] My fruit is better than gold, yea, than fine gold; and my revenue than choice silver.

The revenue or profit provided by possessing lady wisdom is enduring and incomparable. Not even the greatest indicators of wealth in the ANE (purest gold or sterling silver) could produce a better yield than wisdom.

[20] I lead in the way of righteousness, in the midst of the paths of judgment:

Returning to the two ways of life motif, lady wisdom leads according to the standards of the righteousness of God. If you are going to follow wisdom you have to walk where she walks. She does not turn to the right hand or to the left but lives in the middle of the path of justice, "causing man to know the way wherein he should walk" (Psalm 143:8).

[21] That I may cause those that love me to inherit substance; and I will fill their treasures.

Lady wisdom promises that those who follow her down the straight paths of life will be satisfied with the reward of a life well lived, a rich inheritance. Their inheritance, indicative of their success in life, fills their literal treasury, which was measured in herds, crops, clothing, land, precious metals, and children. This inheritance perhaps also fills their proverbial treasury: "Lay up for yourselves treasures in heaven" (Matthew 6:20).

[22] The LORD possessed me in the beginning of his way, before his works of old.

A new theme begins in verses 22-31 as wisdom describes her ancient origins and displays her excellence. Wisdom was possessed or owned or "created" by YHWH "in the beginning," before anything else.

[23] I was set up from everlasting, from the beginning, or ever the earth was.

So, YHWH "set up" or installed lady wisdom in the most favored and honored position before anyone or anything else came into existence so that she could be employed in "helping" YHWH create the universe.

[24] When there were no depths, I was brought forth; when there were no fountains abounding with water.

The preexistence of wisdom is put forth again. Even before man's earliest conception of the creation of the world, before "darkness was upon the face of the deep" (Genesis 1:2), wisdom existed with YHWH.

[25] Before the mountains were settled, before the hills was I brought forth:

What Moses said concerning the eternality of YHWH "before the mountains were brought forth" (Psalm 90:2), wisdom says of herself concerning her ancient origins and involvement with YHWH in the creation of the world.

[26] While as yet he had not made the earth, nor the fields, nor the highest part of the dust of the world.

Continuing to parallel Psalm 90, what is said of YHWH is affirmed of wisdom "or ever thou hast formed the earth and the world" (Psalm 90:2). Wisdom worked with YHWH to create everything, all the mass of the earth's dust.

[27] When he prepared the heavens, I was there: when he set a compass upon the face of the depth:

After touting the preexistence of wisdom, a description of wisdom's role in creation is given. Perhaps this is a reference to wisdom cooperating with God in making the firmament and dividing "the waters which were under the firmament from the waters which were above the firmament" (Genesis 1:7).

[28] When he established the clouds above: when he strengthened the fountains of the deep:

Wisdom was not a bystander at creation but was there working with God when He established the clouds above, suspended in the atmosphere, making the sky capable of sustaining them. And wisdom was there strengthening the springs deep in the earth whose flowing and reflowing can only be attributed to the wisdom of God.

[29] When he gave to the sea his decree, that the waters should not pass his commandment: when he appointed the foundations of the earth:

Wisdom was there when YHWH gave the sea laws that it must observe (not to pass their boundaries, i.e., the seashore) and laid the foundations of the earth. The creation of the earth is compared to the foundation of a building. This familiar metaphor (Job 38:4) is given to meet us on our level since the way creation actually happened is inconceivable to our finite minds.

[30] Then I was by him, as one brought up with him: and I was daily his delight, rejoicing always before him;

Wisdom was the architect of rearing up the "building" called Earth with YHWH. The expression of wisdom rejoicing is meant to denote the ease with which YHWH and wisdom created and the joy their work produced.

[31] Rejoicing in the habitable part of his earth; and my delights were with the sons of men.

In finishing the description of her ancient origins and her role in creation, wisdom found joy in every stage of creation. Her most joyful moment was when "God saw everything that He had made and behold it was very good," when the livable and cultivated portions of land were inhabited by man.

[32] Now therefore hearken unto me, O ye children: for blessed are they that keep my ways.

If mankind, the children of the sons of men, for whom the world was made, would only embrace wisdom, they could return to the harmony and happiness the ancients once had with her. In the conclusion (8:32-36), wisdom again explains to her children the importance of obeying her voice.

[33] Hear instruction, and be wise, and refuse it not.

Now that the sons of men know how great the power of wisdom is and what love she has for them, displayed in creating the world with YHWH for them, they ought to be wise and not ignore her chastening or correction.

[34] Blessed is the man that heareth me, watching daily at my gates, waiting at the posts of my doors.

The idea of a man earnestly watching for wisdom to appear, and not taking a chance of missing her appearance, is comparable to a young man longing for the appearance of his love: "I loved her [wisdom] and sought her from my youth, and I desired to take her for my bride, and I became enamored of her beauty" (Wisdom of Solomon 8:2).

[35] For whoso findeth me findeth life, and shall obtain favour of the Lord.

Those who search and find lady wisdom receive long life, an indication of God's blessing in the world of the Bible (Job 42:17). Continuing with the idea of the young man and lady wisdom's relationship being parallel to that of lovers, this verse states that those who find wisdom obtain favor of YHWH, just like those who find a wife (18:22).

[36] But he that sinneth against me wrongeth his own soul: all they that hate me love death.

The discourse ends with a warning, the reoccurring theme of

choosing between two ways of life, the way of life or the way of death. With a strong expression of individuality, whoever misses the mark and fails to find lady wisdom has no one to blame but himself. The ultimate winner or loser is you.

Proverbs 9

[1] Wisdom hath builded her house, she hath hewn out her seven pillars:

Though we don't have the typical heading "my son," chapter 9 is the fifteenth and last discourse of the first book. This discourse finishes the solid blocks of teaching in the first book and transitions to the short and somewhat isolated discourses in the remainder of the book of Proverbs. This chapter centers on the two choices of rival feasts, perhaps wedding feasts, given separately by wisdom and folly. In preparation for the feast, wisdom has erected a recognizably large and well-built house. The great banquet hall in the courtyard of her house is open to all who are bidden. The house is sturdy, supported by a row of seven pillars symbolizing the perfect completeness and wisdom which supports her edifice (Judges 16:29).

[2] She hath killed her beasts; she hath mingled her wine; she hath also furnished her table.

Counter to the adulteress (7:14), lady wisdom also has her own feast. The menu for her guests is comprised of the best of the best, a royal meal (1 Kings 4:22), consisting of fine meat, wine flavored with spices to improve its flavor, and every side dish imaginable (Matthew 22:4). The table is set, and lady wisdom now waits for those who were bidden to come unto the marriage supper.

[3] She hath sent forth her maidens: she crieth upon the highest places of the city,

As the bride awaits the coming of her guests at her house, her servants (the virgins), following the custom of the day, were sent forth to call them that were bidden to the feast (Matthew 22:3). Effort was made to make the message known to all that the time of the feast had come; they even shouted the message from the rooftops (Matthew 10:27).

[4] Whoso is simple, let him turn in hither: as for him that wanteth understanding, she saith to him,

This is the invitation of lady wisdom. As lady folly invites the simple into her home (9:16), so does lady wisdom. She urges the foolish and ignorant, perhaps "both bad and good" (Matthew 22:10), to turn from their evil ways and partake with her in a sumptuous feast.

[5] Come, eat of my bread, and drink of the wine which I have mingled.

The shocking taboo of receiving and eating with sinners is not an issue for lady wisdom, just as it was not an issue for Jesus the Messiah (Luke 15:2). Addressing those sinners who attended the wedding, wisdom invites them to partake in the "sacraments," bread and wine.

[6] Forsake the foolish, and live; and go in the way of understanding.

As those who partake of eating the Messiah's flesh and drink His blood have eternal life (John 6:54), so those who partake of wisdom's "sacraments" repent of their evil and walk in the light.

[7] He that reproveth a scorner getteth to himself shame: and he that rebuketh a wicked man getteth himself a blot.

Verses 7-10 form a parenthesis and show why wisdom addresses only the foolish and ignorant and not the unredeemable scorner. These verses also teach why the simple should not remain in the company of scorners with the misleading hope of converting them to wisdom since they will only receive a stain on their character.

[8] Reprove not a scorner, lest he hate thee: rebuke a wise man, and he will love thee.

It is foolish for a wise man to reprimand a wicked person since he would only expose himself to the scorner's unbridled rage. But it is prudent for a wise man to rebuke a fellow wise man since it is an act of great kindness (Psalm 141:5).

[9] Give instruction to a wise man, and he will be yet wiser: teach a just man, and he will increase in learning.

It is commanded to literally "give to a wise man." Wise men are to instruct, reprove, correct, etc., fellow wise men since, unlike the scorner, they will be grateful for the criticism that helps them move from immaturity to maturity. The more a wise man learns, the more he loves wisdom.

[10] The fear of the LORD is the beginning of wisdom: and the knowledge of the holy is understanding.

The last discourse ends the way the first discourse started (1:7), with the teacher's basic theme and the motto of the book, the essence of ancient Israelite philosophy, namely that the first step toward wisdom is having a reverential fear of YHWH. This holy knowledge of the fear of YHWH corresponds to the theme from the Joseph account: "This do, and live; for I fear God" (Genesis 42:18).

[11] For by me thy days shall be multiplied, and the years of thy life shall be increased.

The parenthetical insert is over. Wisdom again continues her argument as to why her advice in the preceding verses should be obeyed, namely that she gives long life to her followers (an indication of divine blessing in the world of the Bible).

[12] If thou be wise, thou shalt be wise for thyself: but if thou scornest, thou alone shalt bear it.

This verse is perhaps the strongest expression of individualism in the entire Bible. The sense is that it is beneficial for you to be wise and harmful to you to be wicked since the decisions you make determine how you will succeed or suffer.

[13] A foolish woman is clamourous: she is simple, and knoweth nothing.

In verses 13-18, the conclusion of the discourse, we have a picture of the counter-feast hosted by lady folly. Lady folly is described in the opposite terms of lady wisdom; she is without restraint and has no shame.

[14] For she sitteth at the door of her house, on a seat in the high places of the city,

As lady wisdom summoned men to enter her house for a sumptuous feast, so in like manner lady folly calls out to those passing by her house (which is not built with the pillars of wisdom) to feast with her.

[15] To call passengers who go right on their ways:

All the people in the city are busy going about their daily routines except lady folly, who slothfully and perhaps immorally sits on her "throne" trying to seduce people from what they know is the right thing to do.

[16] Whoso is simple, let him turn in hither: and as for him that wanteth understanding, she saith to him,

Imitating lady wisdom, lady folly offers the same audience an invitation to her feast. Lady folly seems to attract those who are going straight on their ways, minding their own business, who do not have the stamina to stay on the right path but in time of temptation fall away.

[17] Stolen waters are sweet, and bread eaten in secret is pleasant.

Lady wisdom offered meat and wine to her guests, but lady folly only offers bread and water. Lady wisdom invited her guests to a public meal, but lady folly invites her guests to a secret meal. Despite the great discrepancy in the quality of life, lady folly has the charm of being forbidden and therefore the propensity to allure corrupt humanity.

[18] But he knoweth not that the dead are there; and that her guests are in the depths of hell.

Lady folly's house leads the simple man to a mausoleum. She welcomes the simple ones to the underworld, and she is their host. She kindly asks the next fool to step into her house all the way and make room for everyone, as there is no turning back now from hell. This verse's position allows the first portion of Proverbs to end on a shattering climax. Its content corrects the impression that men are saved or lost merely through an isolated impulsive decision to embrace wisdom or salvation. The choice of following wisdom is seen ripening into character and so on into destiny.

PROVERBS 10

[1] The proverbs of Solomon. A wise son maketh a glad father: but a foolish son is the heaviness of his mother.

The new title and different style of arrangement signify a new collection of proverbs. With chapter 10 comes a series of isolated pithy statements and maxims of Solomon which better fit our traditional understanding of the definition of proverbs. Generally speaking, throughout the rest of the book the reader will no longer encounter extended discourses on a particular subject, lengthy poems on the virtues of wisdom, and dramas of a fool in the night. The sense of the verse is that what the son does will have great ramifications on the honor of his family, especially in the slow-paced, tight-knit, conservative society of ancient Israel. In regard to the mother, who is introduced to balance out the maxim, a foolish son, like Esau, is heaviness or "a grief of mind" unto his parents (Genesis 26:35).

[2] Treasures of wickedness profit nothing: but righteousness delivereth from death.

Tainted wealth or perhaps worldly riches in general have momentary pleasure but no lasting value. What does it profit a man if he gains the whole world but loses his own soul (Matthew 16:26)? The point is that only wise living brings satisfaction and can save your life.

[3] The LORD will not suffer the soul of the righteous to famish: but he casteth away the substance of the wicked.

YHWH will not let those perish who honor Him through seeking His righteousness and who do not seek ill-gotten wealth, but rather will add all things unto them (Matthew 6:33). But on the other hand, YHWH does refuse to satisfy the craving of those who are against Him: the wicked.

[4] He becometh poor that dealeth with a slack hand: but the hand of the diligent maketh rich.

There are two different Hebrew words used for hand in this maxim. The lazy person, who soon becomes poor, has a *caph*, an open and ineffective hand; in contrast the hard worker who becomes wealthy has a *yad*, a tense and braced hand ready for intense labor.

[5] He that gathereth in summer is a wise son: but he that sleepeth in harvest is a son that causeth shame.

A wise man is watchful for the best time to act. When the harvest of summer fruits (grapes, figs, pomegranates, etc.) is ready to be reaped, he stores them in the barn. But a fool who literally snores during the short harvest season is a total disgrace. He should not be helped and has no one to blame but himself for his lack of substance.

[6] Blessings are upon the head of the just: but violence covereth the mouth of the wicked.

The contrast is between the visible blessings of YHWH upon the wise (like a good harvest) and the sinister plots of the wicked to attain similar material blessings. The sense is that the wicked are just waiting for the chance to enact their violent intentions in order to be as well supplied as the wise.

[7] The memory of the just is blessed: but the name of the wicked shall rot.

In the ANE, the memory of the deceased righteous man lived on through his good name and even through naming descendants after him. In contrast, the name or destiny of the wicked man rots away like his corpse, for who thinks of naming their child Jezebel or Judas?

[8] The wise in heart will receive commandments: but a prating fool shall fall.

The literal rendering better shows the contrast. The "solid in heart" are happy to be instructed by other wise men, while the fool's "loose lips" babble, and their unwise words fall back on them.

[9] He that walketh uprightly walketh surely: but he that perverteth his ways shall be known.

People with integrity have nothing to hide and therefore walk through life securely. Those who follow the crooked paths of life cannot walk with confidence, knowing they will slip and fall upon the revelation of their secret sins.

[10] He that winketh with the eye causeth sorrow: but a prating fool shall fall.

Winking was a sign of malice or ill intent in the ANE; "he that winketh the eye worketh evil" (Sirach 27:22). This kind of man and he that babbles will come to ruin. The sense is that the actions of a fool are more certain to destroy them than anything anyone else could hope to accomplish.

[11] The mouth of a righteous man is a well of life: but violence covereth the mouth of the wicked.

The words of the wise are compared to a well of water springing up into everlasting life, providing comfort for those who drink of it. The antithesis is that the deceitful words of the wicked intend to harm others.

[12] Hatred stirreth up strifes: but love covereth all sins.

The wicked man in the last verse and the righteous man in this verse both cover sin but for totally different reasons. The wicked man covers his sin because of deceit but the righteous because he forgives (James 5:20, 1 Peter 4:8).

[13] In the lips of him that hath understanding wisdom is found: but a rod is for the back of him that is void of understanding.

The wisdom of a wise man is seen in his wise speech, but the folly of a fool is not only seen in his unwise speech but also in the punishment he brings upon himself because of his unbridled tongue.

[14] Wise men lay up knowledge: but the mouth of the foolish is near destruction.

Wise people store up wise words like their precious treasure so that it can later be used at a proper time. Quite the reverse, nobody knows what foolish words (which bring near or imminent disaster) will come out of the mouth of a fool.

[15] The rich man's wealth is his strong city: the destruction of the poor is their poverty.

The prosperity of the rich affords them the privilege of redeeming themselves from dangers, but the social standing of the poor makes it impossible for them to defend themselves from calamities.

[16] The labour of the righteous tendeth to life: the fruit of the wicked to sin.

The financial earnings of diligent and honest work of the wise have the blessings of God upon them, but the wicked only make money to squander it on sin, thus enabling them to produce more wickedness.

[17] He is in the way of life that keepeth instruction: but he that refuseth reproof erreth.

The wise man who accepts correction from his friends is shown the way of life, but the fool who rejects constructive criticism (which may be embarrassing and hard to act on) will continue to go astray.

[18] He that hideth hatred with lying lips, and he that uttereth a slander, is a fool.

Hiding hatred makes you a liar and a hypocrite because you are speaking and acting to your neighbor in a way contrary to your real feelings. And the man who does the opposite of hiding hatred but gossips is a fool because he also hurts his neighbor.

[19] In the multitude of words there wanteth not sin: but he that refraineth his lips is wise.

Too much talking is bound to lead to gossip and slander and fall short of truthfulness and love, eventually leading to sin. The teacher advises us to be sensible and consider what we say before we speak.

[20] The tongue of the just is as choice silver: the heart of the wicked is little worth.

Menes, who founded the first known dynasty of ancient Egypt around 3100 BC, first set the value of silver at about one quarter the value of gold. The words of the righteous are comparable to this scarce monetary unit, sterling silver. But the value of what proceeds from the heart of the fool is the opposite of choice silver; it is worthless.

[21] The lips of the righteous feed many: but fools die for want of wisdom.

The words of a good man can spiritually nourish and feed many people. The Hebrew word for feed has the idea of guiding as well as nourishing, like a shepherd tending to his sheep. But on the other hand, fools do not have the wisdom to benefit themselves or others.

[22] The blessing of the LORD, it maketh rich, and he addeth no sorrow with it.

Great wealth is not obtained by wisdom and hard work alone but especially by the blessing of YHWH. The sense of the second part of the verse is that the wise man receives riches from YHWH because YHWH has determined that wealth belongs to wise men.

[23] It is as sport to a fool to do mischief: but a man of understanding hath wisdom.

Knowingly and publicly engaging in immoral activity is considered a fun activity for the fool. The wise man finds a thrill in pleasing God by living a wise life; this is as enjoyable to him as folly is to the fool.

[24] The fear of the wicked, it shall come upon him: but the desire of the righteous shall be granted.

Even though the wicked engage freely in immoral activity, they are still afraid of getting the consequences they deserve. But as for the righteous, there is no fear of getting what they deserve from God.

[25] As the whirlwind passeth, so is the wicked no more: but the righteous is an everlasting foundation.

When the storms of life come, the foolish, having no moral or spiritual foundation, are swept away like the house built on sand, but the foundation of the wise stands firm like the house built on the rock (Matthew 7:24-27).

[26] As vinegar to the teeth, and as smoke to the eyes, so is the sluggard to them that send him.

The runner who loiters in delaying the message is compared to two major annoyances in the world of the Bible, sour wine and smoke. In the world of the Bible chimneys were unknown, save a small slot or slots in the wall near the roof where the smoke from the oven would escape (Hosea 13:3).

[27] The fear of the LORD prolongeth days: but the years of the wicked shall be shortened.

Everything someone does proves or disproves their reverential fear of YHWH. The prudent choices of the wise are rewarded with long life, but the foolish choices of the wicked cut their life short.

[28] The hope of the righteous shall be gladness: but the expectation of the wicked shall perish.

The expectations of the righteous are joyful because they have the hope of being fulfilled by God, but the expectations eagerly awaited by the wicked will come to nothing because they do not fear YHWH.

[29] The way of the LORD is strength to the upright: but destruction shall be to the workers of iniquity.

Those with integrity, who walk in the way of YHWH, live a life without fear as they walk safely under the protection of YHWH. The fool who rebelliously goes astray from the path of YHWH will not be protected but rather will be destroyed.

[30] The righteous shall never be removed: but the wicked shall not inhabit the earth.

A godly generation is promised that they will never be deported from their land by an enemy nation as a consequence for incurring the wrath of God; a wicked generation who defies the *torah* of God is threatened with being uprooted into exile (Leviticus 26:33).

[31] The mouth of the just bringeth forth wisdom: but the froward tongue shall be cut out.

As a good tree brings forth good fruit, so the words of the wise bring forth good advice. But the deceitful words of the unwise are like a bad tree that brings forth bad fruit; that tree will be cut off (Matthew 7:17-19).

[32] The lips of the righteous know what is acceptable: but the mouth of the wicked speaketh frowardness.

The words of the wise are in harmony with what would please God and man. On the contrary, the words of the fool are perverse since they have no thought on how their speech might offend God and man.

PROVERBS 11

[1] A false balance is abomination to the LORD: but a just weight is his delight.

Chapter 11 continues the series of isolated pithy statements and maxims of Solomon which better fit our traditional understanding of the definition of proverbs. The repetition of condemning unethical commerce throughout the Scriptures indicates that this kind of dishonesty was occurring frequently in ancient Israel (Amos 8:5). Merchants had stone weights which supposedly matched some national standard (2 Samuel 14:26), yet they used another set of stones marked the same but with different weights to cheat their customers. Because honesty and integrity are the fabric of a godly society, the teacher sets the record straight. YHWH hates deceit.

[2] When pride cometh, then cometh shame: but with the lowly is wisdom.

The first part of the verse repeats the same verb and could literally be translated "pride comes, shame comes." A modern equivalent might be "party hard, die hard." The sense is that if you want to avoid humiliation, don't be proud! Their counterpart, the lowly, are worthy of being recipients of the wisdom of YHWH because of their humble disposition.

[3] The integrity of the upright shall guide them: but the perverseness of transgressors shall destroy them.

God rewards the wise and the unwise. The integrity or innocence of the righteous will be rewarded by being directed in the way of life. God rewards the dishonesty of treacherous people with destruction.

[4] Riches profit not in the day of wrath: but righteousness delivereth from death.

Wealth won't provide protection to the rich man who has earned God's judgment when He visits a nation to judge them. Only wise living can guarantee protection in the day of the Lord's wrath.

[5] The righteousness of the perfect shall direct his way: but the wicked shall fall by his own wickedness.

The righteousness of the complete or whole man will level the way before him on a straight path to life. The wickedness of the wicked will cause him to stumble and fall, crushing him beneath the load of his own sin.

[6] The righteousness of the upright shall deliver them: but transgressors shall be taken in their own naughtiness.

The honesty of just people will rescue them from danger, but the "naughtiness" or ungodly ambition of crooked people ensnares them. The sense of the verse is the old adage "honesty is the best policy."

[7] When a wicked man dieth, his expectation shall perish: and the hope of unjust men perisheth.

There is an expectation for the wise that they will live a long life; but when the wicked dies, their hope of the blessing of long life and lasting influence dies with them. They relied on their own strength to fulfill their worldly desires, and it failed.

[8] The righteous is delivered out of trouble, and the wicked cometh in his stead.

God rescues the godly out of trouble and makes it fall on the wicked instead. There are numerous instances of this maxim in the Bible, such as Daniel's enemies being devoured by the lions instead of him (Daniel 6:24) and Haman being hanged on the gallows that he had prepared for Mordecai (Esther 7:10).

[9] An hypocrite with his mouth destroyeth his neighbour: but through knowledge shall the just be delivered.

With their profane words and lies, the godless draw their trusting neighbor into schemes and corrupt them; but the just, through their wisdom, will be delivered from the deceit of the hypocrite.

[10] When it goeth well with the righteous, the city rejoiceth: and when the wicked perish, there is shouting.

The entire population of a city would celebrate when a godly man was promoted to a high-ranking political position such as king (Zechariah 9:9). They would also celebrate at the vengeance of God upon the death of a wicked ruler who had persecuted them or perhaps had imposed burdensome regulations such as high taxes and forced labor upon the population (Revelation 18:20).

[11] By the blessing of the upright the city is exalted: but it is overthrown by the mouth of the wicked.

Upright citizens are good for a city and make it prosper through their wise actions and perhaps "the blessing" of their prayers, as Abraham prayed for the cities of the plain and temporarily averted their destruction (Genesis 18:23-32). Contrariwise, the words of the wicked tear a city apart. As the saying goes, the only thing necessary for the triumph of evil is for good men to do nothing.

[12] He that is void of wisdom despiseth his neighbour: but a man of understanding holdeth his peace.

The foolish man who is in need of wisdom belittles his neighbor with contemptuous language, but a wise man, even if he doesn't approve of his neighbor's actions, knows how to remain silent and keep the peace.

[13] A talebearer revealeth secrets: but he that is of a faithful spirit concealeth the matter.

A wise person keeps a secret, but the fool who goes around telling secrets destroys his trustworthiness. Levitical laws which include rules against talebearers were given to ensure that there would be no wickedness or confusion such as this in the land of Israel (Leviticus 19:16).

[14] Where no counsel is, the people fall: but in the multitude of counsellers there is safety.

The Hebrew word for counsel comes from the noun "pilot." If there is not wise leadership steering or piloting a country in the way of righteousness, the nation will sink; but there is sure victory in having many godly advisers steer a nation.

[15] He that is surety for a stranger shall smart for it: and he that hateth suretiship is sure.

There's grave danger in putting up security for anyone's debt—much less a stranger. The cosigner can suffer the loss of his property and even his freedom to fulfill the vow made to the creditor. It's safer to never guarantee another person's debt.

[16] A gracious woman retaineth honour: and strong men retain riches.

A woman, by her graciousness or *chen*, that is to say, elegance and beauty, takes and keeps hold of respect, but powerful or aggressive men gain their respect through accumulating wealth. Perhaps the sense is that both honor and riches are worth pursuing, but the means of attaining them—through grace or aggression—are miles apart.

[17] The merciful man doeth good to his own soul: but he that is cruel troubleth his own flesh.

The *chesed*—mercy or kindness—of the wise will come back to bless him: "Blessed are the merciful, for they shall obtain mercy" (Matthew 5:7), just as the cruelty of a fool will come back to curse him. What goes around comes around!

[18] The wicked worketh a deceitful work: but to him that soweth righteousness shall be a sure reward.

The wicked literally work for "wages of falsehood." The sense is that all their labor really brings no reward or fruit to their life. But the reward of the wise who "soweth righteousness" or lives wisely is a long life enjoying the fruits or reward of their labor.

[19] As righteousness tendeth to life: so he that pursueth evil pursueth it to his own death.

Whoever is steadfast in pursuing a righteous life will be rewarded with long life (a sign of the blessing of God), but the fool who pursues a life of evil will bring upon himself the curse of God, having his days cut short.

[20] They that are of a froward heart are abomination to the LORD: but such as are upright in their way are his delight.

YHWH detests the fool, whose heart, the aspect of man with which God is most concerned (1 Samuel 16:7), is "froward"—perverse or distorted. YHWH delights in the wise, whose conduct is blameless before Him.

[21] Though hand join in hand, the wicked shall not be unpunished: but the seed of the righteous shall be delivered.

"Though hand join in hand" is hard to catch the meaning of. It is perhaps a portrayal of two man shaking to make a vow, or it could mean that the following maxim goes from one generation to the next. Some even see this as a reference to the law of retaliation. Regardless, God overlooks no trespass and will not pardon the fool, but the wise will escape the judgment of God.

[22] As a jewel of gold in a swine's snout, so is a fair woman which is without discretion.

A jewel of gold should be understood as a golden nose ring that went through the right nostril and hung down over the mouth. It was an expensive female ornament used from ancient times (Genesis 24:47). As it would be unseemly to adorn an unclean sow with that which was reserved for beautiful women, so is it unseemly for indiscretion to adorn a beautiful woman.

[23] The desire of the righteous is only good: but the expectation of the wicked is wrath.

The righteous long for good, which eventually brings forth the reward of God's blessings. The wicked who only desire evil have nothing to look ahead to and can only expect the judgment of God's wrath. Or perhaps it means that the unfulfillment of the wicked man's hopes angers him.

[24] There is that scattereth, and yet increaseth; and there is that withholdeth more than is meet, but it tendeth to poverty.

The wise man who gives or scatters his money liberally with a bountiful hand becomes even more blessed, whereas the stingy man who hides his proverbial talent in the ground ends up begging.

[25] The liberal soul shall be made fat: and he that watereth shall be watered also himself.

The sentiment of the previous verse is continued here. The "soul of blessing" or the generous man willing to meet an honest need will prosper. Those who water others, a common metaphor for blessing, will themselves be watered.

[26] He that withholdeth corn, the people shall curse him: but blessing shall be upon the head of him that selleth it.

Consumers curse those merchants who hoard their wheat or barley until it reaches an exorbitant price, but they bless the merchant who sells it at the going rate. The wisdom of God is as relevant to the marketplace as to heaven itself.

[27] He that diligently seeketh good procureth favour: but he that seeketh mischief, it shall come unto him.

The wise seek good, literally "in the morning," and because of their diligence are promised to find favor. The Scriptures often depict men of God rising early, implying dedication to a cause (Genesis 19:27). But the fool does not need the same energy and dedication in his search because evil comes to him.

[28] He that trusteth in his riches shall fall: but the righteous shall flourish as a branch.

Using the metaphor of a tree, the fool who trusts in the uncertainty of riches will soon wither away like autumn leaves, but the wise whose trust is rooted in God will flourish like leaves in spring.

[29] He that troubleth his own house shall inherit the wind: and the fool shall be servant to the wise of heart.

Those who bring shame on their families only inherit the wind; that is to say, they get nothing for all their efforts. Their inheritance has been driven away from them because of their shameful behavior. Such a man, the fool, who has forfeited his inheritance will be forced to work as a servant in his family's estate (Luke 15:19).

[30] The fruit of the righteous is a tree of life; and he that winneth souls is wise.

The righteous man, like a tree of life, gives the fruit of goodness and life to those around him. His wise behavior "turns many to righteousness" (Daniel 12:3) by attracting others to himself where they can receive his fruit or example and live.

[31] Behold, the righteous shall be recompensed in the earth: much more the wicked and the sinner.

Since even the righteous receive their due share of the chastisement of God, how much more the guarantee that the ungodly and the sinner will also receive their recompense of divine correction (1 Peter 4:18)!

PROVERBS 12

[1] Whoso loveth instruction loveth knowledge: but he that hateth reproof is brutish.

Continuing the theme of the contrast of the wise and the foolish, the teacher observes that the wise are teachable and want to improve, but the foolish man who is too proud to take advice is compared to an unteachable, base animal.

[2] A good man obtaineth favour of the LORD: but a man of wicked devices will he condemn.

YHWH acquits and justifies the righteous, who are free from evil intentions toward their neighbor, but He convicts and punishes the wicked, who are guilty of planning harm toward their neighbor.

[3] A man shall not be established by wickedness: but the root of the righteous shall not be moved.

The metaphor is of an olive tree. A life characterized by wickedness, planted in loose soil, will never bring stability. A life characterized by righteousness, planted in good soil, will produce deep and strong roots grounded in love, making whatever he does prosper.

[4] A virtuous woman is a crown to her husband: but she that maketh ashamed is as rottenness in his bones.

A virtuous, or literally "of power" wife, a woman of great ability and character as described in chapter 31, is a crown of joy and gladness to her husband, adorning and beautifying his life. On the other hand, a shameful wife is an incurable evil like bone cancer, bringing about the downfall of her husband.

[5] The thoughts of the righteous are right: but the counsels of the wicked are deceit.

The "thoughts" or purposes of the godly are "right," or literally "are judgments"; that is to say, true decisions are the constant purpose of the wise man, while treachery is the purpose that guides the fool.

[6] The words of the wicked are to lie in wait for blood: but the mouth of the upright shall deliver them.

The lies of the wicked are calculated to bring about their intended purpose, to viciously end the lives of their victim; but the words of the godly deliver themselves or perhaps others from the murderous ambitions of the wicked.

[7] The wicked are overthrown, and are not: but the house of the righteous shall stand.

In the world of the Bible, it was believed that a man's life and legacy lived beyond his death through his sons, who would carry on his family name and oversee his land. Perhaps the sense is that the lineage of the wicked or cursed man who did not have male descendants is overthrown, but the dynasty of the righteous, those blessed with sons, survives.

[8] A man shall be commended according to his wisdom: but he that is of a perverse heart shall be despised.

A man who behaves himself wisely wins public admiration: "David went out whithersoever Saul sent him and behaved himself wisely... and he was accepted in the sight of all the people" (1 Samuel 18:5); but a man warped in his words and works is despised.

[9] He that is despised, and hath a servant, is better than he that honoureth himself, and lacketh bread.

The sense is that it is better to be a nobody, not an honored public figure, and yet be doing well enough for yourself that you meet the standards of the day for living a good life (having a servant) than to be living a lie of pretending to be a somebody important when you truly have nothing, not even food to eat.

[10] A righteous man regardeth the life of his beast: but the tender mercies of the wicked are cruel.

The wise farmer cares for the needs of his animals by letting them rest on the Sabbath (Exodus 20:10) and not muzzling the ox when it threshes grain (Deuteronomy 25:4). But the foolish farmer does not recognize that well-cared-for animals produce more and bring higher prices.

[11] He that tilleth his land shall be satisfied with bread: but he that followeth vain persons is void of understanding.

In a contrast between industry and idleness, the wise farmer who spends his time tilling the land will produce a sure return, but the foolish farmer who neglects his business will be reduced to poverty and moral depravity.

[12] The wicked desireth the net of evil men: but the root of the righteous yieldeth fruit.

The Hebrew word translated "net" may also be translated "fortress." So, the sense would be that the wicked desire to fortify themselves through their wicked practices. Or perhaps the sense of the verse is that thieves desire each other's net or loot, but the godly are satisfied with their own fruit.

[13] The wicked is snared by the transgression of his lips: but the just shall come out of trouble.

The wicked are entangled in problems by their self-incriminating speech, but even when the godly fall into a snare set by the wicked, their wise speech and behavior allow them to escape from trouble.

[14] A man shall be satisfied with good by the fruit of his mouth: and the recompence of a man's hands shall be rendered unto him.

A man's words as well as his works bring him either blessings or cursings from God and man. The wise man's words produce great benefits, and his hard work brings financial rewards. In short, you get what you deserve.

[15] The way of a fool is right in his own eyes: but he that hearkeneth unto counsel is wise.

A fool thinks his own way or judgment is correct. The wise do not trust their own unassisted and impetuous judgment, which can be misguided and lead them off course; instead, they listen to the advice of others.

[16] A fool's wrath is presently known: but a prudent man covereth shame.

A fool is quick-tempered and immediately shows his annoyance when reproached; the wise person conceals the injury done unto him, turns the other cheek, and stays cool, calm, and collected.

[17] He that speaketh truth sheweth forth righteousness: but a false witness deceit.

The wise man continually or habitually accustoms himself to only speaking the truth. Therefore, like a witness in court, his speech can be depended upon to execute justice—unlike the fool, whose speech encourages injustice.

[18] There is that speaketh like the piercings of a sword: but the tongue of the wise is health.

The thoughtless and cutting "babblings" of the fool are harmful and reckless, but the soothing words of the wise bring healing to the wounds of those who were attacked by the speech of the reckless fool.

[19] The lip of truth shall be established for ever: but a lying tongue is but for a moment.

The truthful words of the wise stand the test of time, whereas the lies of the fool are momentary, lasting as long as literally "while I wink the eye"; they are not to be feared since they are suddenly discovered and exposed.

[20] Deceit is in the heart of them that imagine evil: but to the counsellers of peace is joy.

Every person fills themselves with something. Deceit fills the heart of the fool who gives evil advice to their neighbor, but joy fills the heart of the wise man who gives sound advice to others.

[21] There shall no evil happen to the just: but the wicked shall be filled with mischief.

Harm, that is to say, the evil consequences that accompany a life of habitual sin, does not come to the wise, but the fool has no peace as their lives are filled with the tumultuous, self-inflicted consequences of their sins.

[22] Lying lips are abomination to the LORD: but they that deal truly are his delight.

An abomination to YHWH is anything that is detestable, unlawful, or repulsive in a ritual or ethical sense. Here YHWH detests lying lips. Those who tell the truth are the object of His delight.

[23] A prudent man concealeth knowledge: but the heart of fools proclaimeth foolishness.

The wise don't always make a show of their great knowledge but sometimes wait until the right opportunity presents itself. The fool, on the other hand, cannot help exposing his ignorance as he aimlessly blabbers his stupidity.

[24] The hand of the diligent shall bear rule: but the slothful shall be under tribute.

Authority is usually not given but taken. The wise man who works hard rises to the top and has the opportunity to become an authoritative leader, but the lazy fool will continue to stay under the authority of the hardworking ruler.

[25] Heaviness in the heart of man maketh it stoop: but a good word maketh it glad.

The cares of this world bring "heaviness," sorrow or fear, and can exact their toll on one's well-being. Worrying only brings dejection and despair, but an encouraging word from a friend can bring relief to their anxiety.

[26] The righteous is more excellent than his neighbour: but the way of the wicked seduceth them.

The godly man "is more excellent," or guides in the right way, or gives good advice to his friends; but the wicked, far from being capable of even morally guiding themselves (much less guide others), lead their friends astray.

[27] The slothful man roasteth not that which he took in hunting: but the substance of a diligent man is precious.

The lazy man makes no effort to gain anything for himself but still feels entitled to eat the finest food—roasted meat—at the expense of others, whereas with the hardworking man, diligence is his precious possession.

[28] In the way of righteousness is life; and in the pathway thereof there is no death.

Once again expressing the theme of two ways of life, a life characterized by righteousness, "through the narrow gate," will certainly lead the wise man to a life of blessings; this path does not lead to condemnation but to justification.

PROVERBS 13

[1] A wise son heareth his father's instruction: but a scorner heareth not rebuke.

The theme of the contrast of the wise and the foolish continues. A wise son is the result of godly parental teaching and the code of the family. The scorner who mocks at sin dismisses those teachings and values that preserve society, thereby undercutting the stability of the family.

[2] A man shall eat good by the fruit of his mouth: but the soul of the transgressors shall eat violence.

The appetite of the wise man hungers for blessings, and blessings he will receive; but the soul, desire, or appetite of the fool hungers for violence, and violence he will receive. The theme "you get what you deserve" may be the most prominent in the book.

[3] He that keepeth his mouth keepeth his life: but he that openeth wide his lips shall have destruction.

Those who control their tongue will have a long life. The teacher advises the son to be sensible and to consider what he says before he speaks, since opening his mouth rashly can quickly ruin everything.

[4] The soul of the sluggard desireth, and hath nothing: but the soul of the diligent shall be made fat.

The lazy fool would love to have the material wealth of the rich man, but he despises the hard work by which those results are obtained. The hard work (not wishful thinking) of the wise will enrich them with the fruit of their own labors.

[5] A righteous man hateth lying: but a wicked man is loathsome, and cometh to shame.

The wise hate every kind of deceit in others, but especially in themselves. However, the wicked don't seem to mind making themselves a stench through their lies. This "loathsome" stench is the same word used for the rotten smell of dead fish in the Nile after the first plague (Exodus 7:21).

[6] Righteousness keepeth him that is upright in the way: but wickedness overthroweth the sinner.

Obedience to the teachings of his father, that is to say, righteousness, will protect the wise son from sinning and slipping off the path of life, but the fool has no moral guide and is subverted by his own sin.

[7] There is that maketh himself rich, yet hath nothing: there is that maketh himself poor, yet hath great riches.

Do not judge by appearances; men act hypocritically in order to gain honor and wealth. One person pretends to have everything yet really has nothing, and another pretends to have nothing yet really has everything.

[8] The ransom of a man's life are his riches: but the poor heareth not rebuke.

The rich are at an advantage because they can easily pay off a ransom for their lives, but the poor are also at an advantage because their poverty makes them immune to ever getting threatened since they have no money to pay off a ransom.

[9] The light of the righteous rejoiceth: but the lamp of the wicked shall be put out.

The blessings of a long life—typified by a burning light—are bestowed upon the wise. But the light or essence of the life produced from the lamp of the wicked soon fails to shine. In the world of the Bible, it was only the totally desolate who could not afford to have a lamp burning in their home overnight, thus the bleak fate of the early death of the fool.

[10] Only by pride cometh contention: but with the well advised is wisdom.

Those who are too proud to take advice from others have an inflated opinion of themselves and are destined for conflict, especially when contending with another person of strong convictions. The wise are open to new ideas and advice.

[11] Wealth gotten by vanity shall be diminished: but he that gathereth by labour shall increase.

Unearned money gotten by vanity or in "a breath"—perhaps by a get-rich-quick scheme like gambling or high-interest usury—has a tendency to quickly disappear, whereas money hard-earned and well-managed by the wise man will grow slowly but surely over time.

[12] Hope deferred maketh the heart sick: but when the desire cometh, it is a tree of life.

The delay in accomplishing some important hope or dream or actually realizing it may never take place makes the heart bitter; but if the dream or desire is finally fulfilled, the result is equivalent to a tree of life, sweet and fulfilling.

[13] Whoso despiseth the word shall be destroyed: but he that feareth the commandment shall be rewarded.

The fools who despise "the word"—religious warnings or instruction—will pay for it as they literally "bring destruction on themselves," but the wise who have a reverence for the word will be rewarded with long life.

[14] The law of the wise is a fountain of life, to depart from the snares of death.

Wise instruction provides nourishment to the soul and is comparable to a life-giving fountain of water. Drinking from this fountain also provides protection, alerting the soul to avoid the deathtraps on the path of life.

[15] Good understanding giveth favour: but the way of transgressors is hard.

A person with good sense is respected by others, but the way of a treacherous person is "hard" and possibly ruinous. Describing the life he leads, the fool, who is callous to the ways of the wise, is on a one-way path to ruin.

[16] Every prudent man dealeth with knowledge: but a fool layeth open his folly.

Wise people "dealeth" or work with knowledge as an artificer fashions brass and iron, deliberating and crafting what they think before they say it; but not so with the fools, who even brag about their foolishness.

[17] A wicked messenger falleth into mischief: but a faithful ambassador is health.

Since the outcome of the message could depended greatly upon the person of the messenger (for example, the eldest servant of the house of Abraham sent to fetch a wife for Isaac; Genesis 24), an unreliable messenger could destroy the intended outcome of the message. On the other hand, a reliable messenger is a source of pleasure both to his Lord and to the party to whom he is sent.

[18] Poverty and shame shall be to him that refuseth instruction: but he that regardeth reproof shall be honoured.

Repeating the theme of taking or rejecting advice, the fool ignores criticism and advice, thus making his lot financial poverty and social disgrace; but the wise man who accepts correction will be honored by both God and man.

[19] The desire accomplished is sweet to the soul: but it is abomination to fools to depart from evil.

It is a sweet feeling when a wise man accomplishes his goal or sees his dream come true; but in spite of the sweetness of a dream fulfilled, fools will not forsake their sin in order that they too may attain the joy of a great accomplishment.

[20] He that walketh with wise men shall be wise: but a companion of fools shall be destroyed.

Since you become like those you spend the most time with, if you associate with the wise you also will become wise from being around their godly words and works; but if you choose to cast your lot in with the fools, then you too will become morally ruined.

[21] Evil pursueth sinners: but to the righteous good shall be repayed.

Sinners bring about their own problems by their own foolish behavior, hence you see trouble chasing them and ultimately overtaking them; but blessings from God reward the wise behavior of the righteous.

[22] A good man leaveth an inheritance to his children's children: and the wealth of the sinner is laid up for the just.

Wise people leave an inheritance, often in antiquity in the form of land, to their grandchildren, but the sinner's wealth, perhaps unjustly acquired land, is taken from their potential heirs and finds its way into the inheritance of the wise.

[23] Much food is in the tillage of the poor: but there is that is destroyed for want of judgment.

The poor farmer who works hard to plow and sow his land may produce a great harvest, but it can all be for nothing if he is not wise enough to properly distribute and sell the crops before they spoil.

[24] He that spareth his rod hateth his son: but he that loveth him chasteneth him betimes.

The rod was a length of tree limb or bush stock and eventually became the symbol of authority and rule for the ancient Israelites (Exodus 4:20). Those who love their children care enough to "chasteneth him betimes" or to discipline him "in the morning," while they still may be rightly influenced.

[25] The righteous eateth to the satisfying of his soul: but the belly of the wicked shall want.

In the cause-and-effect world of the Bible, because YHWH blesses the habitation of the just, the wise always have enough food to eat; but since the curse of YHWH is on the house of the wicked, they are punished with poverty.

Proverbs 14

[1] Every wise woman buildeth her house: but the foolish plucketh it down with her hands.

Written especially with the training of young men in mind, the father presents the son with his potential mate: a wise woman who builds her home through virtue. She is contrasted with a foolish woman who destroys all that wisdom has built with her folly.

[2] He that walketh in his uprightness feareth the LORD: but he that is perverse in his ways despiseth him.

Those with knowledge, the upright, follow the right path because they keep the motto and philosophy of the book: they fear YHWH. But those who despise knowledge, such as the fool, take the crooked path because they do not fear YHWH.

[3] In the mouth of the foolish is a rod of pride: but the lips of the wise shall preserve them.

A fool's proud talk is comparable to a rod, a length of tree limb or bush stock that is used to punish those who are not wise enough to remove themselves from striking distance. The words of the wise keep them safe from the violent outbursts of slander, accusations, etc., present in the fool's speech.

[4] Where no oxen are, the crib is clean: but much increase is by the strength of the ox.

This verse can be understood different ways, but the sense seems to be that without investing in oxen (the necessary instrument for labor and industry), there is nothing to sell or store, but the farmer who does take the risk of investing can expect to gain financial returns.

[5] A faithful witness will not lie: but a false witness will utter lies.

The wise man continually accustoms himself to only speaking the truth. Therefore, like a faithful witness in court, his speech can be depended upon as being truthful—unlike the fool, whose speech is always counted as untrustworthy.

[6] A scorner seeketh wisdom, and findeth it not: but knowledge is easy unto him that understandeth.

A mocker of divine truth who walks after his own lusts also seeks wisdom but never finds it because he searches for it in all the wrong places. On the contrary, knowledge comes easily to those with the fear of God since they understand the primary condition for obtaining true knowledge.

[7] Go from the presence of a foolish man, when thou perceivest not in him the lips of knowledge.

The young man is commanded to leave the presence of a fool since after all the talking back and forth you really carry nothing profitable away with you in the end. It is better to just stay far away and not waste your time.

[8] The wisdom of the prudent is to understand his way: but the folly of fools is deceit.

The sensible understand where they are going and how they are going to get there, but the misguided fool, who thinks he knows everything and can't be told anything, will certainly end up in total disaster.

[9] Fools make a mock at sin: but among the righteous there is favour.

Sin, or "the sin offering," of fools mocks them since all their labor and expense in purchasing their ceremonial offering and bringing it to the priests in the Temple is in vain, since God is not pleased with their offering (Matthew 5:23-24). But the offering of the wise is accepted, providing reconciliation between God and man.

[10] The heart knoweth his own bitterness; and a stranger doth not intermeddle with his joy.

Each person's heart knows its own bitterness better than anyone else, and no matter how hard one tries, no one can totally sympathize with another's sorrows by saying "I know how you feel." In the same way, no one else can fully share the joy in another person's heart.

[11] The house of the wicked shall be overthrown: but the tabernacle of the upright shall flourish.

From an outward appearance the house of the fool seems well-built with deep foundations; but because it is built on wickedness, when storms arise it will have a great fall. But the tent of the righteous, whose outward appearance seems flimsy and vulnerable, because it is staked on righteousness will not fall (Matthew 7:24-27).

[12] There is a way which seemeth right unto a man, but the end thereof are the ways of death.

There is a way of living life that seems right and convenient for the fool; its gate is wide, and its pathway is broad and easy to travel, but it ends with destruction. But the way of living life chosen by the wise is difficult and hard to master; its gate is narrow, and its pathway is hard to travel, but it ends with the reward of life (Matthew 7:13-14).

[13] Even in laughter the heart is sorrowful; and the end of that mirth is heaviness.

Laughter, synonymous with joy, can conceal a sad man's heavy heart for a while, but when the party is over and the laughter subsides, the grief of the man who does not have wisdom still remains.

[14] The backslider in heart shall be filled with his own ways: and a good man shall be satisfied from himself.

Backsliding fools are compared to a stubborn heifer which resists the commands of their master and gets the punishment they deserve, but the wise who are willing to submit to the yoke of their God will receive their reward.

[15] The simple believeth every word: but the prudent man looketh well to his going.

Simpletons have no wisdom or discretion but believe everything they're told, which leads to them making terrible life decisions; but the wise carefully consider the advice given to them before making a decision.

[16] A wise man feareth, and departeth from evil: but the fool rageth, and is confident.

The wise are cautious and try to avoid danger in all matters of thought and practice, but the fool quickly falls into a rage and without thinking plunges headlong with reckless abandonment into his eagerness.

[17] He that is soon angry dealeth foolishly: and a man of wicked devices is hated.

Perhaps the comparison here is between short-tempered people who do foolish things and schemers who are deliberate, plotting evil-doers, provoking others to hate them even more than the impatient fool.

[18] The simple inherit folly: but the prudent are crowned with knowledge.

The reward of living life as a "simpleton" (naïve or open-minded) is receiving the inheritance of foolishness, but the reward of living a life as "the prudent" (shrewd or crafty) is receiving the inheritance of literally being "surrounded or encircled" with wisdom.

[19] The evil bow before the good; and the wicked at the gates of the righteous.

Though victory may be long delayed, wisdom will ultimately prevail against folly. This victory is portrayed with the wicked honoring the righteous in the familiar ANE custom of prostrating themselves as defeated foes at the feet of their conquerors, seeking their mercy, in the city conquered and controlled by the righteous.

[20] The poor is hated even of his own neighbour: but the rich hath many friends.

The poor are shunned and disliked even by those who are supposed to love them, namely their neighbors, because they cannot provide an advancement of anyone's greedy agenda, while the rich, because of the power gained from their connections and hard work, have gained many admirers.

[21] He that despiseth his neighbour sinneth: but he that hath mercy on the poor, happy is he.

The last verse was an observation, and this verse is the moral lesson drawn from it. It is a sin to have contempt for a man based solely on his economic state. The wise turn that sin around into a blessing; they exchange contempt for mercy in their interactions with the less fortunate.

[22] Do they not err that devise evil? but mercy and truth shall be to them that devise good.

The teacher emphatically declares that if you plan to do evil, you will be diverted from the proper course. The word for plan or "devise" has the idea of plowing or engraving, implying both a mental action (thinking of evil) as well as a physical action (causing evil). But if you plan to do good, you will receive unfailing love and faithfulness to accompany you on the path of life.

[23] In all labour there is profit: but the talk of the lips tendeth only to penury.

All hard work guarantees to bring forth a reward, a harvest of 100-fold, 60-fold, or 30-fold of what was originally invested, but the lazy person who just talks about his great ideas is only led into abject poverty.

[24] The crown of the wise is their riches: but the foolishness of fools is folly.

The dividends of hard work and industry and the blessings of God in the form of material wealth adorn the wise man like a royal crown, setting him apart from the fool, whose efforts yield no public adoration but rather foolishness.

[25] A true witness delivereth souls: but a deceitful witness speaketh lies.

Framed in a courtroom setting, a truthful witness confirms the testimony of the innocent defendant, thus clearing the charges against him and saving his life, but a false witness speaks lies to the destruction of the innocent defendant.

[26] In the fear of the LORD is strong confidence: and his children shall have a place of refuge.

Those who have a reverential fear of YHWH (which is the teacher's basic theme and motto of the book) can take refuge within YHWH as an impregnable fortress. In the second part of the verse there is ambiguity as to whose children are provided protection—YHWH's children or the children of the man who fears YHWH.

[27] The fear of the LORD is a fountain of life, to depart from the snares of death.

The fear of YHWH, the essence of ancient Israelite philosophy and the first step toward knowledge, provides the wise man with access to the pure river of the water of life and delivers him from death.

[28] In the multitude of people is the king's honour: but in the want of people is the destruction of the prince.

The honor and majesty of a king cannot exist without a vibrant population of subjects who are responsible for a growing economy, a strong military, and paying taxes. A prince without subjects only has a useless title without power and influence.

[29] He that is slow to wrath is of great understanding: but he that is hasty of spirit exalteth folly.

When a wise man is able to control his anger despite being greatly offended, his patience is put to the test and displayed for all to see; but a quick-tempered man flaunts his anger so all can see that he is indeed a fool.

[30] A sound heart is the life of the flesh: but envy the rottenness of the bones.

When the heart, the seat of all the spiritual, moral, intellectual, volitional, and emotional aspects of man, is at peace with God and man, it leads to a healthy mind and body. Conversely, the sickness of jealousy is like a cancer that riddles the body of the fool.

[31] He that oppresseth the poor reproacheth his Maker: but he that honoureth him hath mercy on the poor.

The fool who harasses the poor is ultimately insulting God, the One who created the poor man. By helping the least of these, a wise man ultimately honors God, doing the good works in His name (Matthew 25:40).

[32] The wicked is driven away in his wickedness: but the righteous hath hope in his death.

The wicked are thrown down to their death by their own misfortune and are therefore no longer able to oppress and persecute the righteous; the righteous trust or hope for the death of the wicked.

[33] Wisdom resteth in the heart of him that hath understanding: but that which is in the midst of fools is made known.

Wisdom is preserved in the heart of the wise man to be accessed and implemented as needed. But wisdom has not only revealed herself to the wise—since even among fools she lets herself be known—because she is not willing that any should perish.

[34] Righteousness exalteth a nation: but sin is a reproach to any people.

The Hebrew word for nation implies much more than a government or political entity. The word can also refer to individuals or groups of people aside from geographic or ethnic considerations. Righteous behavior exalts any people group, while sin brings contempt and ruin upon them.

[35] The king's favour is toward a wise servant: but his wrath is against him that causeth shame.

A king rewards his wise servants, like Joseph (Genesis 41:39-44) and Daniel (Daniel 2:48), by promoting them to positions of influence. But he is angry with those servants who disgrace him, like the butler and the baker, and in his wrath he disposes them (Genesis 40:1-3).

Proverbs 15

[1] A soft answer turneth away wrath: but grievous words stir up anger.

A wise man does not shrink away from confrontation but, having his tongue under control, gives a gentle answer, thus deflecting anger; but a harsh response can stir up tempers like poking a fire.

[2] The tongue of the wise useth knowledge aright: but the mouth of fools poureth out foolishness.

The wise make their knowledge appealing to others by using their words at the right time and in the right place, but the words of a fool work the opposite way. Fools only repel others when they belch out their foolishness.

[3] The eyes of the LORD are in every place, beholding the evil and the good.

"Beholding" is a term often used to describe the task of a watchman (1 Samuel 14:16); this verse portrays YHWH as observing, as it were, from His high tower in heaven above. He is observing both the evil and good actions of man on Earth below (Zechariah 4:10).

[4] A wholesome tongue is a tree of life: but perverseness therein is a breach in the spirit.

The gentle words of the wise are like a tree of life which bears good fruit; the fruit of the tree provides healing and life for those who partake of it. But the deceitful words of the fool accomplish the opposite; they crush the spirit of those who partake of them.

[5] A fool despiseth his father's instruction: but he that regardeth reproof is prudent.

Since readers assume the role of sons who must choose between those values that preserve society and alternative actions that undercut family stability, only a foolish son would despise his father's valuable advice, whereas a wise son learns from correction.

[6] In the house of the righteous is much treasure: but in the revenues of the wicked is trouble.

There is much treasure in the house of the godly because it was gained honestly, thus the blessing of God is upon it. Such treasures would likely be represented in clothing, livestock, and precious stones, common standards of wealth in the ANE (James 5:2-3). But the deceitful pursuit of riches by the wicked only brings the curse of God to their home.

[7] The lips of the wise disperse knowledge: but the heart of the foolish doeth not so.

The reader faces a choice of allegiance: whether to contribute to a godly society by accepting the good advice of the wise or to join the ranks of society's dissidents by harkening to the fool, who does not disperse knowledge.

[8] The sacrifice of the wicked is an abomination to the LORD: but the prayer of the upright is his delight.

The maxim is given to reprimand those who thought they found favor with YHWH by their numerous costly sacrifices when in fact YHWH favored the comparatively inexpensive or "free" sacrifices from the lips of the godly.

[9] The way of the wicked is an abomination unto the LORD: but he loveth him that followeth after righteousness.

YHWH detests the way the wicked live their lives, but on the other hand He loves those who "follow" or pursue after godliness like a predator chases after a prey. This verse gives the reasoning behind the rejection and acceptance of offerings in the previous verse.

[10] Correction is grievous unto him that forsaketh the way: and he that hateth reproof shall die.

Whoever abandons the right path (the good doctrine taught to them by their parents), and thereby deprives their family of its honor, will be severely disciplined. And whoever hates that correction and will not repent of their rebellion will die; in the ANE they could perhaps die at the hands of their parents (Deuteronomy 21:21).

[11] Hell and destruction are before the LORD: how much more then the hearts of the children of men?

If YHWH can see into the depths of the grave and into the far recesses of the bottomless pit so that even they cannot hide any secrets from Him, how much more does He know the condition of the human heart?

[12] A scorner loveth not one that reproveth him: neither will he go unto the wise.

A scorner is a miserable person who derides and ridicules the most sacred truths of God. Because he resists the truth, he resists godly advice; therefore, he deliberately stays away from the wise so as not to prick his seared and guilty conscience.

[13] A merry heart maketh a cheerful countenance: but by sorrow of the heart the spirit is broken.

Since our face is the canvas of our heart, it can easily betray our true feelings. Unless someone has the rare gift of a "poker face," it is easy to perceive when someone has either a glad or a broken heart.

[14] The heart of him that hath understanding seeketh knowledge:

but the mouth of fools feedeth on foolishness.

As the old saying goes, "you are what you eat." A wise person is personified as having a ferocious appetite for knowledge, but the fool on the other hand only fills himself with trash. Garbage in, garbage out!

[15] All the days of the afflicted are evil: but he that is of a merry heart hath a continual feast.

For the despondent in spirit there is no rest as every day seems to bring a different kind of trouble. But for those who are happy in heart, their life is joyful; each day is like one party after another.

[16] Better is little with the fear of the LORD than great treasure and trouble therewith.

Since material possessions cannot bring true happiness, it is better to have a little, with a reverential fear of YHWH, than to have great treasure along with inner turmoil in the house of the wicked.

[17] Better is a dinner of herbs where love is, than a stalled ox and hatred therewith.

In another "better than" proverb, a meal of culinary herbs—which probably refers to a bowl of inexpensive vegetables—with someone you love is better than eating an expensive fattened beast on a special occasion with someone you hate. The menu is inconsequential; what's important is who you are with.

[18] A wrathful man stirreth up strife: but he that is slow to anger appeaseth strife.

A foolish and hot-tempered person who lacks the fruit of patience is quick to start fights, but a wise and cool-tempered person is a peacemaker and has the ability to ease tensions rather than elevate them.

[19] The way of the slothful man is as an hedge of thorns: but the way of the righteous is made plain.

A lazy person's path of life has been blocked with self-inflicted obstacles because of his own lack of the fortitude with which to maintain his own life, whereas the path of the diligent is without obstacles and is evenly graded because of their diligence in maintaining their life.

[20] A wise son maketh a glad father: but a foolish man despiseth his mother.

Sensible children who honor the code of their family bring great honor to their parents, but rebellious children who despise their mother's teachings give them the greatest grief. The mother, whose voice is never audible in the book, still gives additional weight to the warnings against dangerous conduct.

[21] Folly is joy to him that is destitute of wisdom: but a man of understanding walketh uprightly.

Foolish behavior is fun and brings pleasure to those who have no common sense, but a sensible person, despite the strong temptation to go down the wrong path, finds his joy in pleasing God and his parents by walking the straight and narrow path.

[22] Without counsel purposes are disappointed: but in the multitude of counsellers they are established.

Great plans often quickly go wrong because of a lack of planning and a failure to get good advice in the earliest stages, but seeking many recommendations and deliberating over issues brings good plans success.

[23] A man hath joy by the answer of his mouth: and a word spoken in due season, how good is it!

Probably keeping with the theme of sound advice in the previous verse, it is noted that the correct reply to a question is enjoyed by everyone, as well as advice given "in due season," that is to say, at the right time.

[24] The way of life is above to the wise, that he may depart from hell beneath.

Obedience to the teachings of his parents, that is to say, walking upon the way of life, leads the wise son on morally high ground and prevents him from taking the path down to the realm of the dead.

[25] The LORD will destroy the house of the proud: but he will establish the border of the widow.

YHWH uproots the house of those who trust in their own strength to protect themselves, but He establishes the often-disputed rights and property boundaries of the weakest members of ancient Israelite society, the widows.

[26] The thoughts of the wicked are an abomination to the LORD: but the words of the pure are pleasant words.

YHWH hates what is evil and loves what is good. For example, He detests the ill-intended thoughts or plans of the wicked but loves the pure words which proceed from the thoughts of the righteous.

[27] He that is greedy of gain troubleth his own house; but he that hateth gifts shall live.

The foolish man who gains wealth by immoral means only brings God's wrath upon himself and his family, but the wise man who hates what the fool loves, namely bribes, will live a life blessed by God.

[28] The heart of the righteous studieth to answer: but the mouth of the wicked poureth out evil things.

Knowing the power of the tongue, the heart of the wise deliberates and thinks very carefully before making thoughts into speech. This contrasts with the mouth of the fool which, without thought or consideration, spews out nothing but evil words.

[29] The LORD is far from the wicked: but he heareth the prayer of the righteous.

The sense is that YHWH distances Himself from the wicked man so He may not hear his prayer: "Now we know that God heareth not sinners." However, this chasm does not exist between Him and the righteous: "But if any man be a worshipper of God, and doeth his will, him he heareth" (John 9:31).

[30] The light of the eyes rejoiceth the heart: and a good report maketh the bones fat.

"The light of the eyes," or a cheerful countenance, belongs to the person who has just received the greatest news. This overcoming joy and relief deeply affects him all the way down to his bones.

[31] The ear that heareth the reproof of life abideth among the wise.

If the son is wise enough to hearken unto the constructive criticism of his parents and the tribal elders to learn the ways that truly please God, then he will be numbered with them among the wise of his community.

[32] He that refuseth instruction despiseth his own soul: but he that heareth reproof getteth understanding.

Completing the idea of the previous verse, if the son rejects the advice of his elders, he is only harming himself; but if he listens to their advice and correction, then he will grow in his understanding of what pleases YHWH.

[33] The fear of the LORD is the instruction of wisdom; and before honour is humility.

The chapter ends with the teacher's basic theme and the motto of the book, the essence of ancient Israelite philosophy; namely that the first step toward wisdom is having a reverential fear of YHWH. Everything one does proves or disproves one's relationship with or fear of YHWH. The maxim in the second clause seems disconnected from the first, but the general sense is "he that shall humble himself shall be exalted" (Matthew 23:12).

PROVERBS 16

[1] The preparations of the heart in man, and the answer of the tongue, is from the LORD.

We make our own plans and decisions. Studies have shown that the average amount of remotely conscious decisions an adult makes each day equals about 35,000. But in spite of our plans, YHWH's purposes prevail over them all.

[2] All the ways of a man are clean in his own eyes; but the LORD weigheth the spirits.

People can easily deceive themselves to justify their motives for sinning. Only when he measures himself against the righteousness of YHWH does man recognize that he has fallen short of the glory of God.

[3] Commit thy works unto the LORD, and thy thoughts shall be established.

If the son "commits his works," or literally "rolls away his labor unto YHWH" as a burden too heavy to be carried alone, YHWH will

121

encourage his faith. God will honor the man's plan to rely on Him for success by bringing his desires to fulfillment.

[4] The LORD hath made all things for himself: yea, even the wicked for the day of evil.

YHWH has created all things, and by Him all things consist for His divine purposes. He has even made the wicked man, giving him a mind and abilities which could be used for good but which instead are used for evil.

[5] Every one that is proud in heart is an abomination to the LORD: though hand join in hand, he shall not be unpunished.

YHWH detests the proud so much that He will not pardon them "though hand join in hand." This phrase is a portrayal of two men shaking hands to finalize a vow; it signifies that the maxim is a certainty.

[6] By mercy and truth iniquity is purged: and by the fear of the LORD men depart from evil.

Mercy and truth are not atoning for iniquity in man. Only the perfect Sacrifice can atone for man's sin. Rather, this verse points out that you can't pursue sin and righteousness at the same time. By putting on mercy and truth, one will naturally put off iniquity (Ephesians 4:22-24). A reverential fear of YHWH will put a man on the path going the opposite way of evil.

[7] When a man's ways please the LORD, he maketh even his enemies to be at peace with him.

A man who loves his enemies is a man whose actions please YHWH (Matthew 5:44). The adversaries of the wise man will find it difficult to recompense him evil for good, thus resulting in a truce between the parties.

[8] Better is a little with righteousness than great revenues without right.

Since money can buy neither happiness nor the favor of God, it is better to have a little earned honestly and with a clear conscience than to have much earned dishonestly with a guilty conscience and the accompanying fear that this profit could be seized.

[9] A man's heart deviseth his way: but the Lord directeth his steps.

A man "deviseth," which suggests intensity of calculation, his course or direction in life. He prepares his plans with great care, but ultimately God determines whether his desires will be fulfilled and how.

[10] A divine sentence is in the lips of the king: his mouth transgresseth not in judgment.

The true king, like the true prophet, speaks authoritatively with divine wisdom, which is to say with God's verdict. Therefore, as God's representative on Earth, the king must never judge his subjects unfairly.

[11] A just weight and balance are the Lord's: all the weights of the bag are his work.

The repetition of condemning unethical commerce throughout Scripture indicates that it was occurring frequently. Dishonest merchants had stone weights which matched some national standard (2 Samuel 14:26) but on the sly used another set of stones marked the same but with different weights in order to cheat their customers. Because honesty and integrity are the fabric of a godly society, the teacher sets the record straight that YHWH hates deceitful business practices.

[12] It is an abomination to kings to commit wickedness: for the throne is established by righteousness.

The sense of the verse can either mean that a wise king ordained by God to execute justice does not tolerate wicked behavior from his subjects, or perhaps the sense is that life is unbearable for the whole nation when the king behaves wickedly.

[13] Righteous lips are the delight of kings; and they love him that speaketh right.

The previous verse stated what a righteous king hates, and this verse states what he loves, namely advisors and officials, representatives of the king himself, who are not deceitful but honest in their speech.

[14] The wrath of a king is as messengers of death: but a wise man will pacify it.

Continuing a string of verses concerning the ideal king, if the infamous wrath of an ANE king was kindled against you (Daniel 3:19), it was equivalent to having a death threat; therefore, the wise man will try to appease his wrath and live another day. This abuse of power, though common, was contrary to the behavior of an ideal king.

[15] In the light of the king's countenance is life; and his favour is as a cloud of the latter rain.

Finishing the maxims of an ideal king, when the king is exceeding glad, there are blessings for his kingdom. His favor refreshes his subjects like the latter rains in March and April, giving the crops a final good drink before the barley and wheat harvest.

[16] How much better is it to get wisdom than gold! and to get understanding rather to be chosen than silver!

The profits gained from buying wisdom and understanding are greater than the dividends a young man could earn from trading in precious metals. Wisdom makes the young man richer than money ever will.

[17] The highway of the upright is to depart from evil: he that keepeth his way preserveth his soul.

In the world of the Bible, as today, there were different routes for transportation. There was the Great Trunk Route or International Highway following the course of the Fertile Crescent. There were intra-regional routes such as the east-west corridors of the Shephelah which connected the high hill country with the coastal plain. There were footpaths which connected villages. As an ancient highway would lie right before the traveler and could not be mistaken, so the clear duty of the young man is to stay on the main route, thus avoiding the byways that lead to evil.

[18] Pride goeth before destruction, and an haughty spirit before a fall.

The theme of this proverb is continually enforced throughout the book. The sense of the verse is that pride, the sin God most hates (6:16-17), is the underlying cause of men's ruin. In like manner, the parallel phrase states that an arrogant attitude precedes man falling, or better "sliding," to his end.

[19] Better it is to be of an humble spirit with the lowly, than to divide the spoil with the proud.

With another "better than" proverb, the teacher states that it is preferable to live a quiet and modest life with the poor but upright members of society than to enjoy the fruits of the pursuits of the proud. This is because to "divide spoil with the proud," the young man must cast in his lot with them and participate in their risky immoral activities to attain such wealth.

[20] He that handleth a matter wisely shall find good: and whoso trusteth in the LORD, happy is he.

Those who listen to the "matter" or wise "word" of instruction from the teacher, which is rooted or based in the philosophy of the book (the fear of YHWH), will prosper. Similarly, those who trust the teachings of the teacher which are in accordance with the precepts of YHWH will have a joyful life.

[21] The wise in heart shall be called prudent: and the sweetness of the lips increaseth learning.

The wise are recognized by others for their discerning spirit and have the unique ability to communicate their thoughts in sweet language, which increases the appetite of their students to learn.

[22] Understanding is a wellspring of life unto him that hath it: but the instruction of fools is folly.

The teachings of a wise man are an inexhaustible source of life and power; they are as refreshing to his students as a drink of fresh water is to a thirsty traveler. Since fools are unteachable, it is a waste of time to invest time and energy on their education.

[23] The heart of the wise teacheth his mouth, and addeth learning to his lips.

Continuing the theme of sound speech, the wise man, who has God's Word written on the tablet of his heart, uses his heart as the source of his teaching. He does not leave the truth hidden but continually brings it to his lips to teach transgressors God's way.

[24] Pleasant words are as an honeycomb, sweet to the soul, and health to the bones.

The comforting or soothing words of a wise man are comparable to honey, a sweet and highly prized foodstuff in antiquity. The kind words, like honey, help enlighten a man's spirit (1 Samuel 14:27).

[25] There is a way that seemeth right unto a man, but the end thereof are the ways of death.

The way of living life that seems right and convenient for the fool is broad and easy to travel but ends with death, whereas the way of living life for the wise is narrow and its pathway is hard to travel, but it ends with the promise of life.

[26] He that laboureth laboureth for himself; for his mouth craveth it of him.

The maxim signifies that hunger is the strongest incentive to drive the idle soul to find employment. Their stomach, like a beggar, pleads with them to find work in order to quench the insatiable appetite.

[27] An ungodly man diggeth up evil: and in his lips there is as a burning fire.

Belial later became explicitly a name for the devil, who is the father of all such evil qualities (2 Corinthians 6:15). A man of belial creates trouble by digging a proverbial pit for his neighbor as a hunter would for his prey by devising gossip and slander about them; his words are as destructive as an out-of-control fire.

[28] A froward man soweth strife: and a whisperer separateth chief friends.

Continuing the theme of the abuse of language, those who gossip and distort the truth scatter strife abroad as a farmer scatters seeds. These seeds turn into a harvest of gossip which can separate even the best of friends.

[29] A violent man enticeth his neighbour, and leadeth him into the way that is not good.

Harmful people lure their neighbors into a detrimental confederacy, enticing them to participate in their illegal activity for their own greedy end, and thus lead the otherwise simple person down a path that will end in calamity.

[30] He shutteth his eyes to devise froward things: moving his lips he bringeth evil to pass.

Body language, especially the eyes and the lips, were frequently used in the ANE as a means of communicating furtively; in this instance the violent man gives the nonverbal signal for mischief to his allies in a public place.

[31] The hoary head is a crown of glory, if it be found in the way of righteousness.

Gray hair, a symbol of wisdom, honor, and old age (Daniel 7:9), was revered in antiquity and is comparable to a glorious crown adorning the head of the victor. Living to an old age, evidence of the blessing of God upon the wise, is the reward of living a holy life (3:2).

[32] He that is slow to anger is better than the mighty; and he that ruleth his spirit than he that taketh a city.

In another parallel structure verse couched in a "better than" format, the long-suffering man of God is considered braver than a powerful warrior, and the self-controlled man is esteemed as being wiser than the greatest military mind.

[33] The lot is cast into the lap; but the whole disposing thereof is of the LORD.

The lot was a means for determining the will of God before the dispensation of grace. The lot was often cast into the lap, a fold made in the outer garment near the breast for the reception of articles (Luke 6:38). The sense of the verse is that much that we attribute to chance is actually due to the providence of YHWH.

PROVERBS 17

[1] Better is a dry morsel, and quietness therewith, than an house full of sacrifices with strife.

In another "better than" proverb, a peaceful meal with the poor, who cannot even afford wine in which to dip their bread (Ruth 2:14), is better than eating an extravagant but contentious meal with the sumptuous leftovers from the Temple sacrifices (Genesis 31:54). It is likely these strife-ridden meals were notorious for riotous behavior (1 Samuel 1:13).

[2] A wise servant shall have rule over a son that causeth shame, and shall have part of the inheritance among the brethren.

In an example of the superiority of wisdom over foolishness, a wise servant (likely one born in the house of his master; Genesis 17:12) could rise to the highest ranks (Genesis 24:2), even to the rank of inheriting the portion of the firstborn son like Eliezer of Damascus (Genesis 15:3) if his owner was without a son (Numbers 27:4) or if his master's son was an unworthy fool.

[3] The fining pot is for silver, and the furnace for gold: but the LORD trieth the hearts.

As a blacksmith heats a crucible to refine and purify silver and as he heats a furnace for gold (Malachi 3:3), so YHWH sits as a metalsmith before a pot to remove the dross from a man's heart as it passes through fiery trials.

[4] A wicked doer giveth heed to false lips; and a liar giveth ear to a naughty tongue.

A wicked person, which comes from the Hebrew word meaning "raging" or "tumultuous," eagerly listens to gossip, just as liars pay close attention when people slander in order to give them more opportunities to continue their evil disposition.

[5] Whoso mocketh the poor reproacheth his Maker: and he that is glad at calamities shall not be unpunished.

Poverty and misfortune are distributed by the wise council of the will of God. Therefore, those who ridicule the poor because of their low social standing are insulting the One who ordained it. Those who rejoice at the misfortune of others should take heed lest the same thing happen to them.

[6] Children's children are the crown of old men; and the glory of children are their fathers.

The fabric of ANE society was woven around land and family. Male grandchildren bejeweled the patriarch like a crown of glory since they would carry on the stability of the family to the next generation. The family name and rule cannot continue without male children, the pillars of the dynasty, so the pride or glory of sons is that of a long genealogy of godly wise men.

[7] Excellent speech becometh not a fool: much less do lying lips a prince.

Wise words are not fitting for a *nabal*, a wicked fool, since his evil works do not correlate with wise words. In like manner, a wise ruler has no business speaking foolish lies since that would mar his character.

[8] A gift is as a precious stone in the eyes of him that hath it: whithersoever it turneth, it prospereth.

Not making a moral judgment call, the sense of the maxim is simply that people, whether for the right or the wrong motive, give gifts as an effective way to influence others to help them achieve their objective.

[9] He that covereth a transgression seeketh love; but he that repeateth a matter separateth very friends.

Love between friends can continue to prosper when an offended wise man just buries a sin committed against him, but the foolish man who is always bringing up old grievances only separates a friendship.

[10] A reproof entereth more into a wise man than an hundred stripes into a fool.

The maxim is an extreme way of stating that a deserved criticism makes a deeper impression upon a teachable man than the severest punishment makes upon the back of a fool. Lashes or scourging were a type of punishment where the criminal had to lie face down before the judges and receive the number of blows, not to exceed forty, of which he had been deemed worthy. There seems to be no specific offense for which scourging was reserved among the Jews in antiquity.

[11] An evil man seeketh only rebellion: therefore a cruel messenger shall be sent against him.

Only evildoers pursue rebellion against the crown. Since rebels must be exterminated, a cruel messenger, the executioner of the king's wrath, is sent to unmercifully squash out a rebellion. For an example of this, consider Benaiah (1 Kings 2:29), who was sent by Solomon on a deadly task to kill Joab.

[12] Let a bear robbed of her whelps meet a man, rather than a fool in his folly.

As a wise man avoids meeting a vengeful bear robbed of her cubs (2 Kings 2:24), in like manner he should avoid confronting a fool who has less rationality than a wild animal when he is caught in the act of his foolishness.

[13] Whoso rewardeth evil for good, evil shall not depart from his house.

If you repay good with evil, which was the complaint of David against Nabal (1 Samuel 25:21), evil is promised to never depart from your family. This unjust return was an unforgivable offense in the ANE. In the case of the Jews who killed the Lord Jesus, they rightly stated, "His blood be on us, and on our children" (Matthew 27:25).

[14] The beginning of strife is as when one letteth out water: therefore leave off contention, before it be meddled with.

As an ancient Israelite would dig a trench with their foot on the banks of the Nile River to let out a steady flow of water into their garden (Deuteronomy 11:10), so is someone who starts a quarrel; once you let the water or quarrel flow, you can never be sure you can totally stop it before it destroys everything. Once the words or water have been let out, you cannot take them back.

[15] He that justifieth the wicked, and he that condemneth the just, even they both are abomination to the LORD.

Since perversion in the courts was a longstanding problem and apparently a cultural norm in ancient Israel (1 Samuel 8:3), the teacher warns the young man that YHWH hates the abuse of justice.

[16] Wherefore is there a price in the hand of a fool to get wisdom, seeing he hath no heart to it?

Since wisdom cannot be bought even with the highest price, it is senseless to pay riches or "tuition" to a wise teacher (1 Samuel 9:7-8) for him to educate a fool since the fool does not possess a heart for learning.

[17] A friend loveth at all times, and a brother is born for adversity.

A wise man has the blessing of being surrounded by friends and family who support him. A friend is always loyal. This message is repeated and ascends in meaning with the declaration that a brother is there to help in times of the greatest hardship.

[18] A man void of understanding striketh hands, and becometh surety in the presence of his friend.

The foolish man agrees to cosign or guarantee the debt of his friend. The inevitable consequence will be him being legally trapped in a bad deal that could place his freedom and property at his friend's disposal.

[19] He loveth transgression that loveth strife: and he that exalteth his gate seeketh destruction.

Anyone who loves to quarrel loves sin, just like anyone who constructs a large and braggadocious entryway for their home in the world of the Bible invites thievery and disaster. Consider the small, unadorned, and humble entryway one must enter in order to gain access to the glories inside the Church of the Nativity in Bethlehem.

[20] He that hath a froward heart findeth no good: and he that hath a perverse tongue falleth into mischief.

The heart, the aspect of man with which God is most concerned (1 Samuel 16:7), is "froward," that is, perverse or distorted. It will not prosper, just as he who says one thing one time and another thing another time will fail.

[21] He that begetteth a fool doeth it to his sorrow: and the father of a fool hath no joy.

It is painful to be the parent of a *kesil*, a bold and self-confident fool. There is no joy for the father of a *nabal*, a senseless fool who is dull in his mental faculties, since they deprive the family of its honor.

[22] A merry heart doeth good like a medicine: but a broken spirit drieth the bones.

Cheerfulness or joy in the heart is contagious and has the ability to show on a person's countenance. It serves the health of the owner and those around them. A sick spirit, however, can make people physically ill and drag down those around them.

[23] A wicked man taketh a gift out of the bosom to pervert the ways

of judgment.

The wicked judge takes secret bribes to pervert the course of justice. The bosom refers to the folds of the garment, the girdle, in which the money was concealed (Matthew 10:9); from there it could be quickly transferred into the judge's possession to influence his verdict.

[24] Wisdom is before him that hath understanding; but the eyes of a fool are in the ends of the earth.

Sensible people keep their eyes fixed on wisdom; they operate efficiently within realistic boundaries. But a fool's eyes are bigger than his stomach; they go to "the ends of the earth," meaning he does not operate in reality but has plans that are unrealistic and unattainable.

[25] A foolish son is a grief to his father, and bitterness to her that bare him.

The actions of a disobedient son have great ramifications on the honor of a family, especially in the conservative world of the Bible. Again, the mother is introduced to balance out the proverb. A foolish son, like Esau, is bitterness or "a grief of mind" to his parents (Genesis 26:35).

[26] Also to punish the just is not good, nor to strike princes for equity.

"Also" or "another thing" that is not good for the wise is to pervert justice. It must have been common to fine or "tax" obedient subjects for being good citizens and to punish leaders with the greater punishment of scourging for being an honest ruler who would not bow to the immoral pressures of the corrupt establishment.

[27] He that hath knowledge spareth his words: and a man of understanding is of an excellent spirit.

Since too much talking eventually leads to a man offending in word, people with intelligence are renowned for having "an excellent," restrained or cool, spirit; that is to say, they are even-tempered and self-controlled.

[28] Even a fool, when he holdeth his peace, is counted wise: and he that shutteth his lips is esteemed a man of understanding.

Continuing the theme of the virtue of brevity, even fools don't betray their ignorance when they keep their mouths shut. When they are swift to hear and slow to speak, they too seem to work the righteousness of God.

PROVERBS 18

[1] Through desire a man, having separated himself, seeketh and intermeddleth with all wisdom.

The sense of this difficult verse is that an isolated or unfriendly person is not involved in the free exchange of ideas which can profit everyone; they only pursue their own selfish ends and resist any wise advice.

[2] A fool hath no delight in understanding, but that his heart may discover itself.

This continues the warnings against antisocial behavior. Fools have no interest in learning anything that is contradictory to their presuppositions but only want to talk about themselves and their own opinions.

[3] When the wicked cometh, then cometh also contempt, and with ignominy reproach.

When the wicked come into the presence of anyone, their contemptible behavior shows up with them. Despite their shameful conduct they heap abuse on those trying to correct their evil course.

[4] The words of a man's mouth are as deep waters, and the wellspring of wisdom as a flowing brook.

The words of a wise man are not shallow or easily navigated; they must be respected as they are full of depth and meaning. The source or fountain of his wisdom is a rushing stream that never runs dry.

[5] It is not good to accept the person of the wicked, to overthrow the righteous in judgment.

It is not right for a judge to "accept the person" or acquit the case of the guilty by accepting a bribe, which is just as evil as denying justice to the innocent. Both injustices succeed in eroding the people's confidence in the judicial system.

[6] A fool's lips enter into contention, and his mouth calleth for strokes.

The rash and wicked words of a fool end up getting him into constant quarrels. The punishment for his provocative speech is comparable to the severest of punishments, being whipped with the rod of affliction.

[7] A fool's mouth is his destruction, and his lips are the snare of his soul.

This expands the theme of the correct use of the tongue. Fools suddenly become caught in deadly traps like a wild animal, bringing their life into danger by their foolish and self-incriminating speech.

[8] The words of a talebearer are as wounds, and they go down into the innermost parts of the belly.

Rumors and gossip are not like "wounds"—a better translation is that they are "gulped or swallowed down" like the choicest desserts. That is to say, they are quickly and irresistibly consumed, treasured up in the inmost part of the false accuser.

[9] He also that is slothful in his work is brother to him that is a great waster.

A lazy person and a "waster" take different paths in life but end up at the same destination, totally poverty. The lazy person neglects his business, and the waster lives riotously like the prodigal son.

[10] The name of the LORD is a strong tower: the righteous runneth into it, and is safe.

The name of YHWH, signifying all that He is (Exodus 34:5), is comparable in its protection and defense to an Iron Age 2 impregnable fortress. Upon entry, the righteous are safe, or literally "set on high" above the threatening danger below them.

[11] The rich man's wealth is his strong city, and as an high wall in his own conceit.

Continuing the theme of the previous verse, the rich, on the other hand, think of their wealth as their strong defense, imagining that it makes them immune to problems, protecting them like an impenetrable high wall surrounding a city.

[12] Before destruction the heart of man is haughty, and before honour is humility.

The sense of the verse is that the sin of pride or arrogance is the fundamental cause of man's damnation, but the meek or the humble in spirit "shall be exalted" to a position of honor (Matthew 23:12).

[13] He that answereth a matter before he heareth it, it is folly and shame unto him.

To spout off an answer to something before listening to all the facts is the hallmark of an impatient and unwise man; this act brings both shame and confusion upon him and his public reputation.

[14] The spirit of a man will sustain his infirmity; but a wounded spirit who can bear?

The infirm human body can fall back upon the support of its spirit to overcome both physical and spiritual illness; but when the spirit itself is crushed it has no source of strength to support it but crumbles under the pressure of despair.

[15] The heart of the prudent getteth knowledge; and the ear of the wise seeketh knowledge.

The heart of the prudent and intelligent person, their inward mechanism for acquiring knowledge, is personified as always being ready to learn something new. Their ears, which are their outward mechanism for acquiring knowledge, are always open to wisdom.

[16] A man's gift maketh room for him, and bringeth him before great men.

Giving a financial or material gift to a man of distinction can open up doors of opportunity that would otherwise be locked (1 Samuel 10:27). The gift gives the wise man an opportunity to have access to an audience of influential persons to make things happen for his benefit that otherwise would not.

[17] He that is first in his own cause seemeth just; but his neighbour cometh and searcheth him.

The sense of the verse is that the first to plead his side of a lawsuit in court always sounds right and totally convincing until the cross-examination begins. In other words, don't make a verdict until you have heard more than one opinion; there are two sides to every story.

[18] The lot causeth contentions to cease, and parteth between the mighty.

A primary reason for casting lots was to render an impartial, divine, and final decision on significant matters. Once the lot was cast, no one could contend that the decision was the result of human intervention. The casting of lots amounted to consulting God for the answer (16:33) and would therefore ideally stop all arguments (Joshua 14:2).

[19] A brother offended is harder to be won than a strong city: and their contentions are like the bars of a castle.

A brother wronged—intentionally or unintentionally—is more unyielding than the greatest fortified city. Continuing the parallel, the dispute separates them, making it all but impossible to be reconciled.

[20] A man's belly shall be satisfied with the fruit of his mouth; and with the increase of his lips shall he be filled.

A wise man's words bring him blessings from God which satisfy his soul like a great meal would satisfy his belly. Once again, the theme "you get what you deserve" may be the most prominent in the book.

[21] Death and life are in the power of the tongue: and they that love it shall eat the fruit thereof.

The power of the tongue can bring the consequence of death by defiling the whole body just as easily as it can bring the consequence of life by seasoning your speech with salt; either way a man will reap the consequences and eat what it produces.

[22] Whoso findeth a wife findeth a good thing, and obtaineth favour of the LORD.

The fortunes of a man who finds a wife are comparable to the fortunes of a man who finds a buried treasure; he has found her not on his own accord but by the providence of YHWH the matchmaker.

[23] The poor useth intreaties; but the rich answereth roughly.

The lower classes of society have to plead for mercy and humbly beg the rich as the situation presents itself. In contrast, the wealthier classes of society speak to others as they wish, even harshly since they are without fear of the consequences of offending others.

[24] A man that hath friends must shew himself friendly: and there is a friend that sticketh closer than a brother.

Someone who accepts friend requests too easily does so to their own demise, since he must always be concerned with pleasing this throng of so-called friends; but in contrast to the multitude of fake friends there is the blessing of one real friend that lasts.

PROVERBS 19

[1] Better is the poor that walketh in his integrity, than he that is perverse in his lips, and is a fool.

The contrast in this maxim is between the two general classes of ANE society: the haves and the have nots, the poor-but-honest man and the rich-but-dishonest man. The sense is that honesty is the best policy even if it results in poverty.

[2] Also, that the soul be without knowledge, it is not good; and he that hasteth with his feet sinneth.

It is foolish to have zeal about something without having all the necessary information, just as it is foolish to make snap decisions without thinking something all the way through. Both circumstances will lead to mistakes, causing the foolish man to miss the mark of what he was aiming to accomplish.

[3] The foolishness of man perverteth his way: and his heart fretteth against the LORD.

Foolish people have no one to blame for their troubles but themselves since they ruin their lives by their own foolish decisions, but ironically they don't responsibly get angry with themselves because of their miserable life. Instead, they become angry with YHWH for their miserable lot.

[4] Wealth maketh many friends; but the poor is separated from his neighbour.

Having great wealth gives a man the ability to make or attract many "friends" who can help further his agenda, but the poor have even their closest friend desert them since they are perceived as always wanting something from them.

[5] A false witness shall not be unpunished, and he that speaketh lies shall not escape.

The Torah strictly forbids lying: "Thou shalt not swear falsely" (Exodus 20:16) and decreed the severest penalties against a lying witness: "Then shall ye do unto him, as he had thought to have done unto his brother" (Deuteronomy 19:19).

[6] Many will intreat the favour of the prince: and every man is a friend to him that giveth gifts.

Many will literally "stroke the face of the prince" or curry the favor of a public official in the hope of receiving some favor from them, which is another way of saying that gifts make it possible to "pay for play."

[7] All the brethren of the poor do hate him: how much more do his friends go far from him? he pursueth them with words, yet they are wanting to him.

The sense is that if even the relatives of the poor despise them, how much more will their friends despise them? Though the poor pursue or hunt down their family and friends to request help from them, their family and friends totally avoid them.

[8] He that getteth wisdom loveth his own soul: he that keepeth understanding shall find good.

Contrary to someone who hates his own soul (29:24), a wise person will do whatever is necessary to love his own soul. In this verse, that means the wise man will acquire *leb* ("heart"), which is sometimes translated "wisdom." In like manner, he that safeguards "understanding" will find success on his quest for wisdom.

[9] A false witness shall not be unpunished, and he that speaketh lies shall perish.

The Torah strictly forbids lying: "Thou shalt not swear falsely" (Exodus 20:16) and decreed the severest penalties against a lying witness: "Then shall ye do unto him, as he had thought to have done unto his brother" (Deuteronomy 19:19).

[10] Delight is not seemly for a fool; much less for a servant to have rule over princes.

The laws of justice, morality, and society require that the noble, not the foolish, live in luxury, just like it is not fitting for a slave to have dominion over the rightful heir. It is fools and slaves, the lowest classes of society, who think they are entitled to get what they don't deserve.

[11] The discretion of a man deferreth his anger; and it is his glory to pass over a transgression.

Patient people control their temper and do not show their frustration when things don't go their way, and it is to their credit that they don't overreact when offended but have a willingness to overlook wrongs.

[12] The king's wrath is as the roaring of a lion; but his favour is as dew upon the grass.

The inconstant despots of antiquity could instill terror in their subjects as a roaring lion could, or they could be as favorable to them as the morning dew. There are two seasons of the world of the Bible, "summer and winter" (Genesis 8:22). It generally does not rain in Israel from June through September, so the agriculturally based society was reliant on the morning dew to sustain the summer fruits, just as the subjects of the king were refreshed by his acts of kindness.

[13] A foolish son is the calamity of his father: and the contentions of a wife are a continual dropping.

Two unfortunate situations bring the man of a house dishonor: the continued disappointments of his foolish young son and—perhaps related to the behavior of the dishonorable son—the nagging of his wife which wears out his patience.

[14] House and riches are the inheritance of fathers and a prudent wife is from the LORD.

As fathers customarily give their sons an inheritance of houses and wealth, only the providence of YHWH gives a man a sensible and insightful wife, the opposite of the previously mentioned contentious wife.

[15] Slothfulness casteth into a deep sleep; and an idle soul shall suffer hunger.

The consequences of a lazy man's slothfulness bring about life-and-death scenarios as he lets precious opportunities pass him by; waking up he finds himself and perhaps his family at their wits' end because of his lethargy.

[16] He that keepeth the commandment keepeth his own soul; but he that despiseth his ways shall die.

If the son keeps the commandments, that is to say, those values taught by his father and mother that preserved the society of ancient Israel, he will life a long life; but if he despises the teachings of his parents and chooses alternative actions that undercut family stability, it will lead him to an early grave.

[17] He that hath pity upon the poor lendeth unto the LORD; and that which he hath given will he pay him again.

Whoever is kind to the poor is a wise and compassionate man. He is participating in the work of YHWH, and the dividends of his investment are a promise that YHWH Himself will reward him for what he has done (Deuteronomy 15:10).

[18] Chasten thy son while there is hope, and let not thy soul spare for his crying.

The first clause is straightforward: discipline your child while there is still hope for them to be corrected. The second clause can mean either don't beat them to death when punishing them, or perhaps that if children are not disciplined, their parents are a willing contributor to their death.

[19] A man of great wrath shall suffer punishment: for if thou deliver him, yet thou must do it again.

Hot-tempered fools must pay the penalty for their offense in order to learn from their lesson, for if they are continually rescued from their self-inflicted dilemma, their friends or family will have to keep on saving them repeatedly.

[20] Hear counsel, and receive instruction, that thou mayest be wise in thy latter end.

The father exhorts the son to acquire all the advice and instruction he can while he is young so he can be wise the rest of his life. This ancient proverbial wisdom teaches that every effect has a specific cause.

[21] There are many devices in a man's heart; nevertheless the counsel of the LORD, that shall stand.

Of the many plans that occupy the thoughts and intents of a young man's heart, most of them will not stand; but those plans which are in accordance with the will and purpose of YHWH will prevail.

[22] The desire of a man is his kindness: and a poor man is better than a liar.

What really makes a person attractive is the attribute of kindness. An example is given in the second clause: it is better to be a poor man who would be kind and give if he could than a rich liar who promises but doesn't deliver.

[23] The fear of the LORD tendeth to life: and he that hath it shall abide satisfied; he shall not be visited with evil.

The fear of YHWH, the teacher's basic theme and the motto of the book, proves or disproves the young man's relationship with YHWH. If he has a reverential fear, it will lead him to a long, contented life that is protected from harm.

[24] A slothful man hideth his hand in his bosom, and will not so much as bring it to his mouth again.

People eating in the ANE would take food in their hand from the common dish set in the middle of the table (Matthew 26:23). In a hyperbolic expression, the lazy people are so pathetic that they will not even do the necessary work to feed themselves.

[25] Smite a scorner, and the simple will beware: and reprove one that hath understanding, and he will understand knowledge.

The public punishment of an unrepentant scorner will have no avail in making him penitent, but the object lesson might deter the simpleton passing by from committing a similar crime; the wise man, on the other hand, only needs to be verbally criticized to make him repent.

[26] He that wasteth his father, and chaseth away his mother, is a son that causeth shame, and bringeth reproach.

A son who wastes or spoils his inheritance, that is to say, his father's estate, and who subsequently chases away his widowed mother is an embarrassment and a public disgrace because of his shameful behavior.

[27] Cease, my son, to hear the instruction that causeth to err from the words of knowledge.

The son faces a choice of allegiance, whether to contribute to a godly society or to join the ranks of society's dissidents. If the son stops listening to the advice of his father, he will turn his back on the ideology or code of the family.

[28] An ungodly witness scorneth judgment: and the mouth of the wicked devoureth iniquity.

Belial eventually became a name for the devil himself (2 Corinthians 6:15). An ungodly witness in court makes a mockery of justice; he is literally a belial. Such are wicked men; iniquity to them is like food and water, without which they cannot exist.

[29] Judgments are prepared for scorners, and stripes for the back of fools.

The certainty of punishment is the fate of the scorner who derides, ridicules, and mocks the things of God. So it is also with the fool, whose backs are made to be lashed with the rod of corporal affliction.

PROVERBS 20

[1] Wine is a mocker, strong drink is raging: and whosoever is deceived thereby is not wise.

In every instance drunkenness produces victims. Wine produces victims who deride, ridicule, and scoff at that which is good; and wine mingled with different herbs and spices, which was much more intoxicating than regular wine (Isaiah 5:22), produces the victims of a bloody brawl. Those led astray by alcohol do not use reason and therefore cannot be considered wise.

[2] The fear of a king is as the roaring of a lion: whoso provoketh him to anger sinneth against his own soul.

Encounters with lions were apparently common in antiquity (1 Samuel 17:34, 1 Kings 13:24, 2 Kings 17:25). Lions are mentioned in over half (37) of the books of the Bible and are described as living in forests (Jeremiah 5:6), thickets (Jeremiah 4:7), mountains (Song of Songs 4:8), and desert places (Isaiah 30:6). The fierce attributes and characteristics of an angry lion are compared to the fury of an angry ANE despot. To rouse his anger is to risk having him execute you (Esther 7:10).

[3] It is an honour for a man to cease from strife: but every fool will be meddling.

Avoiding either a physical or verbal altercation by controlling your temper and tongue is truly a characteristic of wise living since only fools insist on starting a fight when they become offended or angry.

[4] The sluggard will not plow by reason of the cold; therefore shall he beg in harvest, and have nothing.

After the early rains have finished around the end of November, the industrious farmer will start plowing and sowing the barley and wheat seeds to be harvested in the late spring. This work is hard, and the temperature outside is the lowest of the year, usually in the high 40s or low 50s. The fool will retreat inside to a warm fire for momentary gratification but will miss the harvest and reap nothing.

[5] Counsel in the heart of man is like deep water; but a man of understanding will draw it out.

The good advice of a man lies deep within his heart like water lies deep beneath the ground at the bottom of a well, but only a wise person knows how to use a proverbial bucket to draw out that wisdom like the Queen of Sheba did from King Solomon (1 Kings 10:1).

[6] Most men will proclaim every one his own goodness: but a faithful man who can find?

Many people are willing and able to announce their good intentions, especially in times of need, but in reality it is practically impossible to find "friends" who will actually do what they promised.

[7] The just man walketh in his integrity: his children are blessed after him.

The righteous man who lives a holy life and instills good doctrine into his children by his words and works makes them respect him. As his kids mimic him, they too walk in integrity and have a blessed life.

[8] A king that sitteth in the throne of judgment scattereth away all evil with his eyes.

It was expected in ancient Israel that the wisdom of God was in the king to do judgment; therefore when the king sat in judgment he weighed all the evidence, distinguishing the bad from the good before making a just decision (1 Kings 3:28).

[9] Who can say, I have made my heart clean, I am pure from my sin?

Since the heart, the inner control center of man (4:23), is deceitful above all things and is desperately wicked (Jeremiah 17:9), the rhetorical question in this maxim implies the answer "no one."

[10] Divers weights, and divers measures, both of them are alike abomination to the LORD.

The repetition of condemning unethical commerce throughout this book indicates it was occurring frequently in ancient Israel (11:1, 16:11). Merchants had stone weights which supposedly matched some national standard (2 Samuel 14:26). Dishonest merchants used another set of stones marked the same but weighing a lesser amount. Because honesty and integrity are the fabric of a godly society, the proverb sets the record straight that YHWH hates deceit.

[11] Even a child is known by his doings, whether his work be pure, and whether it be right.

Since most people do not live up to their words, their works prove they are not faithful men (20:6). It is the same with children; it isn't what they say that proves their faithfulness but their actions.

[12] The hearing ear, and the seeing eye, the LORD hath made even both of them.

Together, hearing and seeing are the best ways of determining what is true and false. From a distance with your eyes, an observed person might seem wise, but upon closer inspection with your ears you may well discover that they are a fool. If what you hear concurs with what you see, you have that which is truth (1 John 1:3).

[13] Love not sleep, lest thou come to poverty; open thine eyes, and thou shalt be satisfied with bread.

The repetition of condemning the fate of the sluggard throughout this book indicates its common occurrence in ancient Israel (12:11, 19:15). An overarching philosophy of the book is that you reap what you sow, and perhaps it is no clearer displayed than here; laziness results in poverty, and hard work results in wealth.

[14] It is naught, it is naught, saith the buyer: but when he is gone his way, then he boasteth.

This proverb is a perfect picture of haggling in the bazaar or marketplace. The buyer haggles over the price, saying, "It's worthless," but then brags about getting a bargain after the transaction.

[15] There is gold, and a multitude of rubies: but the lips of knowledge are a precious jewel.

The young man's wise speech is to be esteemed more valuable than even precious metals or "rubies," a descriptive word used to denote precious stones in general in the marketplace of daily life.

[16] Take his garment that is surety for a stranger: and take a pledge of him for a strange woman.

The proverb is probably more advice to moneylenders than condemnation for cosigners (6:1-5). Wise creditors should require collateral, such as the garment for those foolhardy enough to cosign a debt for a stranger (Exodus 22:26).

[17] Bread of deceit is sweet to a man; but afterwards his mouth shall be filled with gravel.

Stolen bread tastes sweet at first (9:17), but the consequences taste terrible. Perhaps the prison food contained grit which stuck to the grain as it was baked in the hot ashes of the fire, thus the bread tasted like dust and pebbles.

[18] Every purpose is established by counsel: and with good advice make war.

It was common practice in the ANE, and even today, for leaders to deliberate long and hard over military operations. Herodotus mentions when Xerxes laid the plans for his military invasion of Greece: "Xerxes, being about to take in hand the expedition against Athens, called together an assembly of the noblest Persians, to learn their opinions, and to lay before them his own designs" (*History of the Persian Wars*, 7:8).

[19] He that goeth about as a talebearer revealeth secrets: therefore meddle not with him that flattereth with his lips.

Since a gossiper goes around telling secrets, the teacher warns the son to avoid anyone who cannot keep their mouth shut. Levitical law includes rules against talebearers to ensure that this type of foolish behavior would have consequences (Leviticus 19:16).

[20] Whoso curseth his father or his mother, his lamp shall be put out in obscure darkness.

The blessings of a long life—typified by a burning light—are bestowed upon those who honor their parents (Exodus 20:12). But the light or essence of the life produced from the lamp of the wicked who insult their parents will be snuffed out. In the world of the Bible, it was only the totally desolate who could not afford to have a lamp burning in their home overnight, thus the bleak fate of the early death of the fool who curses his parents (Exodus 21:17).

[21] An inheritance may be gotten hastily at the beginning; but the end thereof shall not be blessed.

An inheritance obtained too early in life is not a blessing in the end because man is prone to waste his substance with riotous living —exemplified in the parable of the Prodigal Son (Luke 15:11-32)—or perhaps the sense of the maxim is that an inheritance gained unjustly will end unjustly, exemplified in the trials of the life of Jacob. Or maybe an inheritance gained quickly ends disastrously, exemplified in the inheritances of Gad, Reuben, and the half-tribe of Manasseh who were quickly absorbed into the surrounding people groups of Transjordan. Or perhaps the sense is that inherited wealth is not appreciated like wealth earned by hard work.

[22] Say not thou, I will recompense evil; but wait on the LORD, and he shall save thee.

When offended the normal reaction is to do unto others as they have done unto you, so the teacher implores the student not to commit his cause to the cycle of revenge but to wait in the hope that YHWH will recompense tribulation to those that trouble the saints.

[23] Divers weights are an abomination unto the LORD; and a false balance is not good.

The recurrence of condemning unethical commerce throughout this book indicates that it was occurring frequently (11:1, 16:11, 20:10). Not only could weights be compromised but so could scales, perhaps by adjusting the position of the loads to the seller's advantage. The sense is that YHWH detests cheating others.

[24] Man's goings are of the LORD; how can a man then understand his own way?

Since YHWH directs our steps, He prepares our course with great care and ultimately determines whether our desires will be fulfilled and how. So, why fret and fuss about trying to understand everything along the way since YHWH's will is being accomplished?

[25] It is a snare to the man who devoureth that which is holy, and after vows to make inquiry.

Do not trap yourself by making rash religious promises and only later counting the cost. Of course, this folly is exemplified in the hasty and awful vow of Jephthah. In the portion concerning the law of vows in the Torah, it clearly states the gravity of such a declaration (Numbers 30:2).

[26] A wise king scattereth the wicked, and bringeth the wheel over them.

Though the agricultural order is reversed from the cultural norm, a wise king is compared to an industrious farmer, who is able to discern between the good and the evil, the wheat and the chaff, and to destroy the wicked (Amos 1:3).

[27] The spirit of man is the candle of the LORD, searching all the inward parts of the belly.

The lamp of YHWH, which is that which bears witness and accuses men of their sin, is comparable to our spirit or perhaps our conscience. The ancient Israelites thought of their conscience as a lamp lighting up the inward portions of themselves to prevent their thoughts from getting too dark.

[28] Mercy and truth preserve the king: and his throne is upholden by mercy.

The honorable attributes of wise living, *hesed* or faithfulness, loyalty, love, or mercy and *emet*—which is similar to our word amen, meaning accuracy or truth—are exhibited in the king's judgment, thus upholding or securing his government.

[29] The glory of young men is their strength: and the beauty of old men is the gray head.

Each part of age has its own excellence. Young men naturally take pride in their physical strength, but the gray hair of wisdom and experience exhibit another kind of strength—the endurance of a life well lived.

[30] The blueness of a wound cleanseth away evil: so do stripes the inward parts of the belly.

Continuing the theme of attaining wisdom and experience, men learn wisdom at different paces and by different methods. The sense of the proverb is that sometimes foolish people have to learn the lessons of life the hard way—by physical punishment—in order to purify their heart.

PROVERBS 21

[1] The king's heart is in the hand of the LORD, as the rivers of water: he turneth it whithersoever he will.

The comparison here is taken from artificial irrigation, an easily understood illustration in the agriculturally based society of ancient Israel (Deuteronomy 11:10). As the farmer has control over the flow and direction of the water supply when he digs irrigation channels, so YHWH has total control over the thought and practice of a monarch, even though it appears that he has no superior.

[2] Every way of a man is right in his own eyes: but the LORD pondereth the hearts.

People easily deceive themselves in order to justify their ways, but YHWH weighs man's words and works in the scales or balances of His truth; He alone has the authority to issue a verdict on what is right or wrong.

[3] To do justice and judgment is more acceptable to the LORD than sacrifice.

This verse does not mean that YHWH (who Himself instituted the sacrificial system) ridiculed the prescribed sacrifices but instead that YHWH valued moral obedience with ritual obedience. The concept of this verse is found in the writings, historical books, and prophets (Psalm 51:16-17, 1 Samuel 15:22, Hosea 6:6, respectively).

[4] An high look, and a proud heart, and the plowing of the wicked, is sin.

Perhaps this references the popular reaping and sowing philosophy; since the wicked sow the seeds of conceit and pride in all their endeavors, their harvest is not accepted by YHWH but is condemned as sin.

[5] The thoughts of the diligent tend only to plenteousness; but of every one that is hasty only to want.

Here we have directly opposed ideas: careful planning and hard work which leads to prosperity versus rashness which leads to poverty. The recurrence throughout this book of encouraging hard work with the promise of dividends indicates its value in ancient Israelite society (12:11, 13:11, 14:23).

[6] The getting of treasures by a lying tongue is a vanity tossed to and fro of them that seek death.

The attainment of wealth in an unjust manner is compared to two things: a fleeting, momentary mist which vanishes and a deadly trap. The wicked eventually get what they deserve as they pay for their greed with their own lives.

[7] The robbery of the wicked shall destroy them; because they refuse to do judgment.

The violence of the wicked results in them being "destroyed," which can mean either being caught up like fish in a net or perhaps sawn asunder like the enemies of David (1 Chronicles 20:3). In either case, the wicked will be destroyed because they refuse to do what is right.

[8] The way of man is froward and strange: but as for the pure, his work is right.

The way of life or conduct of an evil man is "froward" or perverted and "strange" or criminal, taking him wherever his evil desires lead. This is contrasted with the way of life for the good man, which is upright and innocent.

[9] It is better to dwell in a corner of the housetop, than with a brawling woman in a wide house.

Offering advice on how to deal with a bad domestic situation, the teacher recommends living on a corner of the roof—which was certainly plausible in antiquity (1 Samuel 9:26), though you could be exposed to inclement weather—rather than sharing a dry and comfortable four-room house with a quarrelsome wife.

[10] The soul of the wicked desireth evil: his neighbour findeth no favour in his eyes.

Evil people wish evil on others because their hearts are fully set in them to do evil (Ecclesiastes 8:11). They are so wicked that they hate everyone: friends, family, and even their neighbors. The whole world is against them, and they are to be shown no mercy.

[11] When the scorner is punished, the simple is made wise: and when the wise is instructed, he receiveth knowledge.

The punishment of an unrepentant scorner will not avail in making him repent, but seeing that scorner being given the punishment might deter the simpleminded from committing a similar crime; the wise man, on the other hand, only needs to be instructed to become all the wiser.

[12] The righteous man wisely considereth the house of the wicked: but God overthroweth the wicked for their wickedness.

The righteous man is not jealous but carefully considers the prosperity of his wicked neighbor; he understands how worthless all their ill-gotten worldly success is because of the divine destruction which awaits them.

[13] Whoso stoppeth his ears at the cry of the poor, he also shall cry himself, but shall not be heard.

To those who do not help the poor, a twofold divine recompense awaits them. They will suffer the same fate of poverty as the poor, and when they cry out for help in time of need, they will be shown no mercy.

[14] A gift in secret pacifieth anger: and a reward in the bosom strong wrath.

The power of privately given gifts to calm a man's anger is best exemplified by the wisdom of Abigail, who gave David and his men presents to stay them from executing her foolish husband, Nabal (1 Samuel 25:18).

[15] It is joy to the just to do judgment: but destruction shall be to the workers of iniquity.

The righteous are highly pleased when justice prevails, whether in court, in the government, or elsewhere. Justice is opposed to the unrighteous, who are terrified when truth is put into action since it reveals their evil deeds.

[16] The man that wandereth out of the way of understanding shall remain in the congregation of the dead.

The person who strays from the path of wisdom illustrated by the maxims of this book will end their foolish life condemned in the company of the dead, in contrast to the wise, who rest in the land of the living (2:21).

[17] He that loveth pleasure shall be a poor man: he that loveth wine and oil shall not be rich.

Those who live a lifestyle above their financial means end up becoming poor since they waste their substance with riotous living, illustrated in the very costliness of fine feasting, good wine (John 2:10), and expensive oil or perfume (John 12:3).

[18] The wicked shall be a ransom for the righteous, and the transgressor for the upright.

God at times rescues the godly and makes their judgment return on the head of the wicked. This is best exemplified in the account of Haman, who was hanged on the gallows that he had prepared for Mordecai (Esther 7:10).

[19] It is better to dwell in the wilderness, than with a contentious and an angry woman.

Again, offering advice on how to deal with a bad situation, it is recommended to live in the *erets* (in a solitary place without shelter) until things calm down than to share a luxurious home with a quarrelsome wife and make a bad situation worse.

[20] There is treasure to be desired and oil in the dwelling of the wise; but a foolish man spendeth it up.

The wise, whose wealth can be a sign of God's blessing upon them because they have worked hard and made wise plans, have thought ahead and stored up wealth. The fool, on the other hand, has nothing saved since he doesn't think ahead but only lives for today. He is one disaster away from financial ruin.

[21] He that followeth after righteousness and mercy findeth life, righteousness, and honour.

The teacher's objectives and methods outlined in 1:2-6—namely, cultivation of the mind and training in ethical principles by the use of proverbs—will lead the young man to a good life characterized by righteousness and honor.

[22] A wise man scaleth the city of the mighty, and casteth down the strength of the confidence thereof.

The sense of the maxim is the superiority of skill over force, brains over brawn in warfare. This is exemplified in the account of Gideon and his 300 men defeating the hordes of Midianites and Amalekites in the Valley of Jezreel with shofars (rams' horns), empty pitchers, and lamps (Judges 7:16-25).

[23] Whoso keepeth his mouth and his tongue keepeth his soul from troubles.

Giving more advice on the power of speech (12:13, 13:8, 18:21), the wise man, who has the ability to guard his tongue (to know when to speak and when not to speak), guards his life from misfortune.

[24] Proud and haughty scorner is his name, who dealeth in proud wrath.

Essential to the being, existence, and character of a person in the world of the Bible was their name. Since a person is exemplified by their name, those who act with insolent pride are named "Proud," "Haughty," and "Scoffer."

[25] The desire of the slothful killeth him; for his hands refuse to labour.

The longing of a sluggard is to have the same standard of living as the hardworking man despite the fact that he would have to work. Because he refuses to labor, this will be the death of him since he will starve or resort to crime to satisfy his cravings.

[26] He coveteth greedily all the day long: but the righteous giveth and spareth not.

The unrighteous are always greedy for more, but the righteous, on the other hand, receive great joy when giving to those who truly need charity, which does not include the previously mentioned sluggard who refuses to labor.

[27] The sacrifice of the wicked is abomination: how much more, when he bringeth it with a wicked mind?

The proverb is given to rebuke those who thought they had found favor with YHWH by their numerous costly sacrifices despite their evil motives. YHWH values moral obedience with ritual obedience (Matthew 5:23-24).

[28] A false witness shall perish: but the man that heareth speaketh constantly.

The Torah decreed the severest penalties against a lying witness (Deuteronomy 19:19). Therefore, the false witness would perish for the crime of perjury, but a credible witness, on the other hand, will be allowed to live on and speak.

[29] A wicked man hardeneth his face: but as for the upright, he directeth his way.

The sense is that a wicked person has to put up a bold appearance or bluff their way through life in order to get people to believe them, whereas the words and works of a wise man speak for themselves.

[30] There is no wisdom nor understanding nor counsel against the LORD.

There is no human wisdom in opposition to YHWH, there is no mortal understanding to be compared to His, and there is no earthly planning that can be opposed to His divine will (1 Corinthians 3:19).

[31] The horse is prepared against the day of battle: but safety is of the LORD.

In connection with the previous verse, though the earthly planning for battle has been considered and implemented, the military victory does not come by natural might or power—personified by the war-horse—but by the divine will of YHWH.

PROVERBS 22

[1] A good name is rather to be chosen than great riches, and loving favour rather than silver and gold.

The father advises the son to seek a name or personal honor over great riches (Ecclesiastes 7:1) since being nameless or having a bad name in the ANE would destroy your existence (Job 30:8). He also counsels him that having grace with people, which demonstrates your honor, is prized by the wise more than the greatest material possessions. The same maxim also appears in inter-testament Jewish wisdom literature: "Have regard to thy name; for that shall continue with thee above a thousand great treasures of gold" (Sirach 41:12).

[2] The rich and poor meet together: the LORD is the maker of them all.

The rich and the poor have nothing in common except one thing: YHWH made them both. YHWH does not "regard the rich more than the poor. For they all are the work of his hands" (Job 34:19).

[3] A prudent man foreseeth the evil, and hideth himself: but the simple pass on, and are punished.

There are numerous examples of the wise foreseeing danger and taking the necessary precautions: Noah, Lot, the Israelites during the plagues of Egypt. In contrast, the simpleton goes blindly on and suffers the deadly consequences.

[4] By humility and the fear of the LORD are riches, and honour, and life.

Humility and the fear of YHWH, the teacher's basic theme and the motto of the book, pay as their dividends material wealth, personal honor, and the satisfaction of living a long life—life the way it is supposed to be.

[5] Thorns and snares are in the way of the froward: he that doth keep his soul shall be far from them.

Corrupt people, people who joined the ranks of society's dissidents, walk a thorny and treacherous road compared to the wise, who guard their soul by avoiding the traps that ensnare the fool.

[6] Train up a child in the way he should go: and when he is old, he will not depart from it.

The sense of the maxim is that parents should teach a child in accordance to the child's way (the child's nature, inclination, and aptitude for learning). Since they are reared in accordance with their individualities, their peculiarities will become honed to usefulness and serve them well in life on the way or path of life they choose.

[7] The rich ruleth over the poor, and the borrower is servant to the lender.

The way the world turns dictates that the rich rule over the poor; the poor must do their bidding and be subject to their cruelties. In like manner, the borrower is at the mercy of the moneylender and must comply with every desire of his master; he must satisfy him before he can satisfy himself or his family.

[8] He that soweth iniquity shall reap vanity: and the rod of his anger shall fail.

Revisiting the popular theme "what you reap is what you sow," those leaders who plant the seeds of injustice throughout the course of their reign will one day reap a harvest of disaster. The effect will be that their reign of terror will come to an end, like the Babylonians (Isaiah 14:6) and Assyrians (Isaiah 30:31).

[9] He that hath a bountiful eye shall be blessed; for he giveth of his bread to the poor.

A special blessing is designated upon those who literally have a "good eye," or are generous to those who are destitute. Those being helped are poor not because they are lazy but by the casting of YHWH's lot.

[10] Cast out the scorner, and contention shall go out; yea, strife and reproach shall cease.

Three benefits or results come from driving out a scoffer from your life (a scoffer being someone who derides and ridicules truth): strife (arguments), quarreling, and verbal insults will cease.

[11] He that loveth pureness of heart, for the grace of his lips the king shall be his friend.

The person who lives a life of righteousness is described as possessing an excellent quality: having grace on their lips. The reward of having such a virtue is being promoted to advisor of the king.

[12] The eyes of the LORD preserve knowledge, and he overthroweth the words of the transgressor.

The watchful eye of YHWH's providence protects and defends those whose words and works glorify Him; He frustrates the treacherous plans or intentions the wicked have devised against these worshippers.

[13] The slothful man saith, There is a lion without, I shall be slain in the streets.

No excuse is beyond the realm of possibility no matter how remote it may be, whether being eaten by a lion in the countryside or murdered in the streets; any excuse will be used by a lazy person in order for them to avoid the rigors of hard work.

[14] The mouth of strange women is a deep pit: he that is abhorred of the LORD shall fall therein.

A method YHWH uses to punish men who anger Him is to have immoral women, who use their smooth talk as bait, trap them in a pit. Literal pits were deadly traps dug by hunters for their prey.

[15] Foolishness is bound in the heart of a child; but the rod of correction shall drive it far from him.

The very nature of children is corrupted. They are naturally self-willed, and the primary remedy for correcting such rebellion is afflicting them with the rod so that wisdom can be learned. The rod was a length of tree limb or bush stock; it eventually became the symbol of authority and rule for the ancient Israelites (Exodus 4:20).

[16] He that oppresseth the poor to increase his riches, and he that giveth to the rich, shall surely come to want.

The immoral man who gets rich by oppressing the poor, whether it be through usury or extortion, and the immoral man who bribes the rich for his own manipulative greed will themselves end up destitute.

[17] Bow down thine ear, and hear the words of the wise, and apply thine heart unto my knowledge.

Verses 22:17–24:34 contain the third collection of proverbs. 22:17-21 is as much a conclusion to the preceding collection as it is an introduction to the next collection. This next section features a different style of speech, usually two or three or more verses connected together, instead of the previous method in the second collection of isolated and independent maxims. This third section begins with a strong imperative for the son to pay attention and listen carefully with his outward (ears) and inward (heart) mechanisms for learning the wise counsel of his father.

[18] For it is a pleasant thing if thou keep them within thee; they shall withal be fitted in thy lips.

This verse is the reason the exhortation was given in the previous verse, namely that the son would treasure the words of his father—the code of his family—enough to memorize them so that they may ornament his person inside (heart) and out (lips).

[19] That thy trust may be in the LORD, I have made known to thee this day, even to thee.

The effect of hiding these maxims in his heart is that the son may call them up and meditate upon them, having them rest on his lips, which causes him to joyfully trust in YHWH, which is the only way to a blessed life.

[20] Have not I written to thee excellent things in counsels and knowledge,

Some suggest this verse can also be rendered "have I not written for you thirty 'sayings' with knowledgeable counsel?" These thirty sayings which constitute this third collection of proverbs (22:17-24:34) are a textbook where normal life settings are addressed with the intent of helping the student move from immaturity to maturity. Perhaps the thirty sayings correlate to the ancient Hebrew calendar of thirty-day months (Revelation 12:6). In 1902 Macalister discovered the Gezer calendar, a school exercise written in classical Hebrew from the 10th century. The small limestone tablet reflects the true agricultural cycle of the land of Israel. The calendar deals with twelve months; these were sectioned into four periods of two months each and four periods of only one month each. The months had thirty days each.

[21] That I might make thee know the certainty of the words of truth; that thou mightest answer the words of truth to them that send unto thee?

The student has achieved a primary objective of the teacher; he has learned the sayings of the teacher so accurately that he can return them verbatim. When the time comes, he can give the same answer as the teacher might have given, thus continuing the ideology and philosophy of ancient Israelite wisdom literature by teaching others also (2 Timothy 2:2).

[22] Rob not the poor, because he is poor: neither oppress the afflicted in the gate:

22:22-23 make up the first grouping of the sayings of the wise. This cluster condemns exploiting the poor. The teacher commands the student not to rob the poor just because he can nor to exploit them in court, which could be done since they could not afford a good defense lawyer.

[23] For the LORD will plead their cause, and spoil the soul of those that spoiled them.

The reason for the exhortation in the previous verse is given here. The courtroom scene continues with YHWH as the Defender of the poor, eager to judge those who commit the heinous sin of exploiting those who cannot defend themselves.

[24] Make no friendship with an angry man; and with a furious man thou shalt not go:

22:24-25 make up the second grouping of the sayings of the wise. As with the previous wise saying, the first verse in the pair gives the exhortation: don't befriend angry people nor associate with hot-tempered people.

[25] Lest thou learn his ways, and get a snare to thy soul.

Giving the reason for the exhortation, the teacher warns the student to avoid foolish companions since his good manners would be corrupted by their evil manners and he would end up being just like them, losing his life.

[26] Be not thou one of them that strike hands, or of them that are sureties for debts.

22:26-27 make up the third grouping of the sayings of the wise. The son is warned that if he puts up security for a friend's debt or agrees to guarantee the debt of a stranger, the inevitable consequence will be him being legally trapped in that bad deal.

[27] If thou hast nothing to pay, why should he take away thy bed from under thee?

If the son should fall into the trap of cosigning, nothing will stop the creditor from collecting the debt. Even the unthinkable can happen; his bed can be snatched from under him (Exodus 22:27).

[28] Remove not the ancient landmark, which thy fathers have set.

22:28 is the fourth saying of the wise. Landmarks were inscribed stones on which the boundaries of fields (private property), districts, and even nations were defined (Genesis 31:51-52). To remove a landmark was a grave offense (Deuteronomy 19:14). Their removal is also used symbolically of overturning ancient customs and mannerisms (Job 24:2).

[29] Seest thou a man diligent in his business? he shall stand before kings; he shall not stand before mean men.

22:29 is the fifth saying of the wise. Someone skilled or prompt in their work will be noticed. They will not be wasted working a mundane job in the presence of ordinary people but will serve or minister in the arena of the highest importance, in the court of the king (Genesis 41:46).

PROVERBS 23

[1] When thou sittest to eat with a ruler, consider diligently what is before thee:

23:1-3 make up the sixth grouping of the sayings of the wise. The father warns the skilled or prompt son whose work is noticed that when he is promoted and dines with a ruler, he should pay close attention not to what but who is before him, namely, that his host is not an equal.

[2] And put a knife to thy throat, if thou be a man given to appetite.

The son must restrain himself by any means necessary when dining in the presence of his superiors so as not to offend the king by anything he says or does. So, he should eat as if he has a knife to his throat.

[3] Be not desirous of his dainties: for they are deceitful meat.

Ending this wise saying, the father warns the son not to fall into the trap of craving the delicacies of a royal feast lest he lose his discretion. The choice foods of the author, King Solomon, included oxen from the fattening pens, pasture-fed cattle, and sheep or goats, as well as deer, gazelles, roe deer, and choice poultry (1 Kings 4:22-23).

[4] Labour not to be rich: cease from thine own wisdom.

23:4-5 make up the seventh grouping of the sayings of the wise. The father exhorts the son not to wear himself out trying to get wealthy (John 6:27). As the son is to restrain himself from eating too much royal food, so he is to restrain himself from a life devoted to obtaining wealth.

[5] Wilt thou set thine eyes upon that which is not? for riches certainly make themselves wings; they fly away as an eagle toward heaven.

The reason for the exhortation in the previous verse is because of the fleeting and momentary nature of earthly riches. What a man has spent a lifetime amassing can disappear in the blink of an eye.

[6] Eat thou not the bread of him that hath an evil eye, neither desire thou his dainty meats:

23:6-8 make up the eighth grouping of the sayings of the wise. The hazard here is the "hospitality" of a stingy and perhaps wealthy host who resents the guests at his banquet because their meal costs him money.

[7] For as he thinketh in his heart, so is he: Eat and drink, saith he to thee; but his heart is not with thee.

The son is warned that such a host is a deceiver since his warm greetings and conversation belie the thoughts and intents of his heart. His evil mind begrudges the money spent on the feast as he thinks about how much the guests are costing him.

[8] The morsel which thou hast eaten shalt thou vomit up, and lose thy sweet words.

The whole course of events at a banquet hosted by the above-mentioned stingy man is nauseating, enough to make you "vomit." Any attempts at praising the host are a waste of time; you will "lose your sweet words." The teacher warns the son to avoid attending such a banquet.

[9] Speak not in the ears of a fool: for he will despise the wisdom of thy words.

23:9 is the ninth saying of the wise. "Sweet words" are also lost on a fool, so the father warns the son to not waste his breath on explaining the virtues of wisdom to a fool, "to cast his pearls before him," since they will only ridicule his wise advice anyway.

[10] Remove not the old landmark; and enter not into the fields of the fatherless:

23:10-11 make up the tenth grouping of the sayings of the wise. Both land and family, the two staples of ANE society, are mentioned in this maxim. Landmarks were inscribed stones on which the boundaries of private property handed down as an inheritance were demarcated (Genesis 31:51-52). Such portable landmarks could be moved slowly but surely over time, seizing the inheritance of "the fatherless." To remove a landmark was a grave offense (Deuteronomy 19:14).

[11] For their redeemer is mighty; he shall plead their cause with thee.

The reason the son is not to cheat his defenseless neighbor is because YHWH Himself is their kinsman redeemer, the closest relative responsible for the welfare of the widow and her children. YHWH will put right what once went wrong for these people.

[12] Apply thine heart unto instruction, and thine ears to the words of knowledge.

23:12 is the eleventh saying of the wise. The maxim is a strong imperative that implores the son to devote his inner (heart) and outer (ears) mechanisms for learning the code of his family, the parental advice given in the proverbs.

[13] Withhold not correction from the child: for if thou beatest him with the rod, he shall not die.

23:13-14 make up the twelfth grouping of the sayings of the wise. For parents perhaps wounded by past experiences of physical or emotional abuse, encouragement is needed for them to not withhold calm, appropriate physical correction when their children need to be disciplined (13:24). So, the teacher comforts the parents that moderate physical correction will not harm them (29:15).

[14] Thou shalt beat him with the rod, and shalt deliver his soul from hell.

Far from harming the child, the parent is doing the child the greatest service by spanking them; this reasonable consequence for young children teaches them vital self-discipline and respect for authority. The loving and definite boundaries parents set for their kids provide a safe atmosphere for growth. The "rod" ideally drives out rebellion which could have led to an early grave. The rod was a length of tree limb or bush stock (Exodus 4:20).

[15] My son, if thine heart be wise, my heart shall rejoice, even mine.

23:15-16 make up the thirteenth grouping of the sayings of the wise. The son must choose between those values that preserve society, the code of his family, and alternative actions that undercut family stability. If the son is wise, it will give his father no greater joy (3 John 1:4).

[16] Yea, my reins shall rejoice, when thy lips speak right things.

By honoring his father with "right" or straight speech, which is indicative of his righteous behavior, the wise son causes his parents to celebrate—compared to the parents of fool whose hearts grieve (10:1).

[17] Let not thine heart envy sinners: but be thou in the fear of the LORD all the day long.

23:17-18 make up the fourteenth grouping of the sayings of the wise. The father warns the son when he sees those set up that work wickedness not to be envious of the success which comes from their earthly wisdom but instead to have a reverential fear of YHWH, which is the first step in getting wisdom from above.

[18] For surely there is an end; and thine expectation shall not be cut off.

The son is promised that it is not vain to serve YHWH and that he will be rewarded for fearing YHWH all day long, in good times and bad. His hope will not be disappointed since he will receive the kind of reward that makes the temporal earthly riches of the sinner pale in comparison.

[19] Hear thou, my son, and be wise, and guide thine heart in the way.

23:19-21 make up the fifteenth grouping of the sayings of the wise. The heading "my son" brings us back to the style of the first collection of the book of Proverbs. Many of the thirty groupings give parental advice to children. The chief literary device is that of a father speaking to a son, thus reinforcing an ideology, the code of the family. In some respects, the subject manner of the thirty groupings is characteristic of the teachings of the entire book of Proverbs.

[20] Be not among winebibbers; among riotous eaters of flesh:

The son is warned not to carouse with drunkards or feast with gluttons. A consistently disobedient son was like a drunkard or glutton, depriving the family of its honor. Acknowledging the shame associated with such licentious living, the Torah permitted capital punishment for such rebellious children (Deuteronomy 21:20-21).

[21] For the drunkard and the glutton shall come to poverty: and drowsiness shall clothe a man with rags.

Many dangers threaten the young man, but two stand out in this grouping: the seductive invitation to sensual pleasure from both eating excessively and drinking alcohol. So, the father warns the son of the results of such debauchery—namely, abject poverty.

[22] Hearken unto thy father that begat thee, and despise not thy mother when she is old.

23:22-25 make up the sixteenth grouping of the sayings of the wise. The son must choose between those values taught by his father that preserve society and alternative actions that undercut family stability. And a mother's voice, although never audible in this book, gives additional weight to the father's warnings against dangerous conduct.

[23] Buy the truth, and sell it not; also wisdom, and instruction, and understanding.

Truth, which is described under the title's wisdom, instruction, and understanding, is to be obtained at any cost. Truth is taught to the son by the father throughout the book in the form of proverbs, warnings, riddles, and puzzling questions.

[24] The father of the righteous shall greatly rejoice: and he that begetteth a wise child shall have joy of him.

The father of godly children has cause for great joy as his children, who have been brought up in the fear and admonition of YHWH, move from immaturity to maturity. What a pleasure to have children who are wise (3 John 1:4)!

[25] Thy father and thy mother shall be glad, and she that bare thee shall rejoice.

If the son learns self-discipline, the right time to act, the advantages of breaking free from the cycle of revenge, the necessity of speaking at crucial times and the folly of doing so in some circumstances, the dangers of initiating violence, the advantage of intellectual discussion, and so on, he will give his parents tremendous joy.

[26] My son, give me thine heart, and let thine eyes observe my ways.

23:26-28 make up the seventeenth grouping of the sayings of the wise. The chief speaker of the book, the father, speaks to the son, reinforcing an ideology—the code of the family. We the readers, like the son, must choose between those values that preserve society, "my ways," and alternative actions that undercut family stability.

[27] For a whore is a deep ditch; and a strange woman is a narrow pit.

An immoral woman is like a hunter, using her smooth talk and sex appeal as bait to trap foolish men in a ditch or pit, like the deadly trap prepared by a hunter. All who fall therein will by no means escape.

[28] She also lieth in wait as for a prey, and increaseth the transgressors among men.

Lying in wait brings the idea of an ambush or of attacking by surprise. The adulteress has her prey, the simple one, in her net. Not giving him time to reflect, she immediately overcomes him. She either adds him to the list of her cliental, or perhaps the sense is that she continually adds to her methods of deception to lure men into her trap.

[29] Who hath woe? who hath sorrow? who hath contentions? who hath babbling? who hath wounds without cause? who hath redness of eyes?

23:29-35 make up the eighteenth grouping of the sayings of the wise. From the sin of sexual immorality, the teacher transitions to condemning drunkenness. This grouping or song is the most comprehensive description of the negative effects of alcohol in Scripture.

[30] They that tarry long at the wine; they that go to seek mixed wine.

This verse answers the previous questions of who has anguish, sorrow, is always fighting, is always complaining, has unnecessary bruises and bloodshot eyes; it is those who linger over wine and "seek" or test out "mixed wine." which some thought improved the taste: "Wine mixed with water makes a delightfully tasty drink" (2 Maccabees 15:39).

[31] Look not thou upon the wine when it is red, when it giveth his colour in the cup, when it moveth itself aright.

As he spoke concerning the adulteress, so the father warns the son not to be deceived by the attractiveness of wine, by its vivid color, sparkle, and touch. He warns him, perhaps from past experience, of the danger of its allure.

[32] At the last it biteth like a serpent, and stingeth like an adder.

Once the buzz of the wine wears off, the hangover comes and everything hurts. The end of wine is compared to the poison of a deadly snake, which overcomes the entire body and produces deadly results.

[33] Thine eyes shall behold strange women, and thine heart shall utter perverse things.

The companion of drunkenness, sexual immorality, tempts the young man to look for women to fornicate with, all the while speaking terrible things he never would utter if he were in his right mind.

[34] Yea, thou shalt be as he that lieth down in the midst of the sea, or as he that lieth upon the top of a mast.

The dazed and confused condition of the drunkard is compared to a sailor trying to keep his balance on the deck of a ship in a mighty tempest. The drunk is as foolish as someone who would try to sleep at the top of the mast. He is exposed to all kinds of deadly dangers but is seemingly ignorant of them all.

[35] They have stricken me, shalt thou say, and I was not sick; they have beaten me, and I felt it not: when shall I awake? I will seek it yet again.

The song ends with the alcoholic momentarily awakening out of his stupor to tell himself that when he sobers up, he will once again drown himself in wine despite all the side effects previously mentioned.

PROVERBS 24

[1] Be not thou envious against evil men, neither desire to be with them.

24:1-2 make up the nineteenth grouping of the sayings of the wise. The father warns the son that when he sees those whose success comes from their earthly wisdom, he should fight his natural impulse of wanting to become like them.

[2] For their heart studieth destruction, and their lips talk of mischief.

The reason for not envying evil men is that their wealth and power are temporary and come from immoral means. Their hearts plot violence in their pursuit to become rich, and their words are always causing trouble for others while financially benefiting themselves. The wisest course of action is to have no fellowship with such unfruitful workers of darkness.

[3] Through wisdom is an house builded; and by understanding it is established:

24:3-4 make up the twentieth grouping of the sayings of the wise. In contrast to the previously mentioned foolish living, wise living constructs the life and dynasty of a wise man. Its foundations are established on discretion or common sense.

[4] And by knowledge shall the chambers be filled with all precious and pleasant riches.

Via wise living, homes are built, established, and furnished with every good thing. The homes of the wise are blessed with extraordinarily great wealth, which is the result of the blessing of YHWH coupled with their hard work and adherence to the maxims of this book.

[5] A wise man is strong; yea, a man of knowledge increaseth strength.

24:5-6 make up the twenty-first groupings of the sayings of the wise. A wise man is rooted and established in strength, and "increases" or grows stronger and stronger over time, accomplishing greater things than others can in their own strength.

[6] For by wise counsel thou shalt make thy war: and in multitude of counsellers there is safety.

It was common practice in the ANE for leaders to deliberate over military operations. Herodotus mentions that when Xerxes laid the plans for his military invasion of Greece, "[He], being about to take in hand the expedition against Athens, called together an assembly of the noblest Persians, to learn their opinions, and to lay before them his own designs" (*History of the Persian Wars*, 7:8). The Hebrew word for counselors comes from the noun "pilot." If there is not wise leadership steering or piloting a country on its way to war, the results will be disastrous.

[7] Wisdom is too high for a fool: he openeth not his mouth in the gate.

24:7 is the twenty-second saying of the wise. Wisdom is beyond the reach of fools. Therefore, among the leaders at the city gate, the cultural, political, and administrative center of the city, fools had nothing worthwhile to contribute to the benefit of their society.

[8] He that deviseth to do evil shall be called a mischievous person.

24:8-9 make up the twenty-third grouping of the sayings of the wise. A person who plans evil will get a reputation as a troublemaker, which would be impossible to shake in the slow-paced, conservative, tight-knit society of ancient Israel.

[9] The thought of foolishness is sin: and the scorner is an abomination to men.

The "thought" or schemes of a fool "who devises to do evil" are sinful and detested by everyone. Once again, the relation between sin and folly, as between wisdom and righteousness, is emphasized.

[10] If thou faint in the day of adversity, thy strength is small.

24:10 is the twenty-fourth saying of the wise. Man has no way of testing his true strength until he is in trouble. Similarly, Jeremiah states, "If racing against mere men makes you tired, how will you race against horses?" (Jeremiah 12:5).

[11] If thou forbear to deliver them that are drawn unto death, and those that are ready to be slain;

24:11-12 make up the twenty-fifth grouping of the sayings of the wise. The son is told to rescue those who are unjustly sentenced and are in clear and present danger of death, perhaps by giving a true witness at their trial.

[12] If thou sayest, Behold, we knew it not; doth not he that pondereth the heart consider it? and he that keepeth thy soul, doth not he know it? and shall not he render to every man according to his works?

Continuing the train of thought, the father exhorts the son that he is his brother's keeper and tells him not to excuse himself by saying "I didn't know my neighbor was in trouble." God understands all hearts and will repay us in accordance with what we deserve.

[13] My son, eat thou honey, because it is good; and the honeycomb, which is sweet to thy taste:

24:13-14 make up the twenty-sixth grouping of the sayings of the wise. This grouping is an exhortation to the study of wisdom using the analogy of honey. The only sweet foodstuffs in the world of the Bible were natural sugars like fructose produced by fruits like dates, apricots, and grapes, or else the honey produced by bees.

[14] So shall the knowledge of wisdom be unto thy soul: when thou hast found it, then there shall be a reward, and thy expectation shall not be cut off.

Wisdom, like honey, is "good" and "sweet" to the soul. Wisdom should be as desirable to the student as honey, filling him with a "reward" or bright future and expectations that will not be cut short.

[15] Lay not wait, O wicked man, against the dwelling of the righteous; spoil not his resting place:

24:15-16 make up the twenty-seventh grouping of the sayings of the wise. The teacher warns us not to wait in ambush like a thief to raid the resting place or house of the godly, since YHWH "blesses the habitation of the just" (3:33).

[16] For a just man falleth seven times, and riseth up again: but the wicked shall fall into mischief.

The godly may end up in trouble often in their lives, which is the expectation of their enemies, but unlike the wicked, the godly will get up again, disappointing their foe. It's pointless to try and harm the godly since YHWH delivers them, and the new result is the expiry of the wicked.

[17] Rejoice not when thine enemy falleth, and let not thine heart be glad when he stumbleth:

24:17-18 make up the twenty-eighth grouping of the sayings of the wise. Concerned with vindictiveness, the teacher warns the son not to rejoice when calamity strikes his enemies—which will eventually happen (24:16)—but instead to "love his enemy" (Matthew 5:44).

[18] Lest the LORD see it, and it displease him, and he turn away his wrath from him.

The reason the son is not to rejoice over the misfortunes of his enemy is because YHWH will be unhappy with him and will punish him for gloating by turning His divine anger away from his enemy (and possibly onto the son).

[19] Fret not thyself because of evil men, neither be thou envious at the wicked;

24:19-20 make up the twenty-ninth grouping of the sayings of the wise. The father warns the son for the third time in this collection about the dangers of envying those who tempt God by amassing great wealth through immoral means (23:17, 24:1).

[20] For there shall be no reward to the evil man; the candle of the wicked shall be put out.

The light or essence of the life produced from the lamp of the evil man soon fails to shine. In the world of the Bible, it was only the very poor who could not afford to have a lamp burning in their home over-night—thus the bleak future of the fool.

[21] My son, fear thou the LORD and the king: and meddle not with them that are given to change:

24:21-22 make up the thirtieth and final grouping of the sayings of the wise. The father ends the thirty sayings with a warning and the essence of ancient Israelite philosophy, namely, that the first step toward knowledge is having a reverential fear of YHWH in heaven. The son is also warned to have a holy fear toward the most powerful person on Earth beneath, namely the king, and not to join company with those who think differently.

[22] For their calamity shall rise suddenly; and who knoweth the ruin of them both?

The reason the son is to not have fellowship with rebels is because punishment from the theocratic government ruled by YHWH through a divinely appointed king is bound to destroy those who do not fear the Lord and the king.

[23] These things also belong to the wise. It is not good to have respect of persons in judgment.

24:23-34 include an unsystematic collection of maxims titled "Further Sayings of the Wise." It functions as an appendix to the third collection of the book. The wise author(s) of the book start by stating that it is evil to judge someone on appearance rather than on merit.

[24] He that saith unto the wicked, Thou are righteous; him shall the people curse, nations shall abhor him:

Developing the previous clause, when the judge who is supposed to be sentencing the wicked instead exonerates them, his name and reputation will be cursed by the whole community.

[25] But to them that rebuke him shall be delight, and a good blessing shall come upon them.

It will go well for those public officials who convict those who are guilty. Rich blessings will be showered on the just judge by their countrymen, in contrast with the cursings showered on the crooked judge.

[26] Every man shall kiss his lips that giveth a right answer.

The kiss to another man's cheek, beard, hands, or feet was the greatest token of affection, greeting, or reverence (Matthew 26:49). As welcoming as a kiss of friendship was in antiquity, so was an honest answer welcome.

[27] Prepare thy work without, and make it fit for thyself in the field; and afterwards build thine house.

The father advises the son to plan well before he undertakes the massive responsibility of purchasing a piece of property. The son needs to test the land to determine if it is suitable for producing crops before he commits to settling there.

[28] Be not a witness against thy neighbour without cause; and deceive not with thy lips.

The father warns the son never to talk about any of his friends' shortcomings behind their backs unless he has sufficient reason. He is not to be known by others as having a love for malice or gossip.

[29] Say not, I will do so to him as he hath done to me: I will render to the man according to his work.

When offended, the normal reaction is to do unto others as they have done unto you (Judges 15:11), so the father advises the son not to commit himself to the vicious cycle of revenge but to live in the hope that vengeance belongs to YHWH.

[30] I went by the field of the slothful, and by the vineyard of the man void of understanding;

The third collection of the book of Proverbs ends with a drama (24:30-34), an extended description which shows what happens to the lazy fool. The scene unfolds through the narration of the author, who describes what he saw as he walked past the unmaintained field and vineyard of an ancient Israelite farmer.

[31] And, lo, it was all grown over with thorns, and nettles had covered the face thereof, and the stone wall thereof was broken down.

The field and the vineyard were the two most important components of the farmer's care. These plots of land needed constant attention if they were to remain productive to the farmer (Isaiah 5:1-2). The vineyard of the lazy farmer was overgrown with nettles, covered with weeds, and its walls were broken down. The walls were meant to protect the vines from wild animals or travelers who would otherwise consume the fruit. The condition of the property was indicative of the work ethic of its owner.

[32] Then I saw, and considered it well: I looked upon it, and received instruction.

Having walked past this property in the high hill country of Judah, the author Solomon thought upon it and let it sink into his heart and learned wisdom, a moral lesson, from the folly of the lazy farmer, which is given in the next verse.

[33] Yet a little sleep, a little slumber, a little folding of the hands to sleep:

Here the father quotes the lazy farmer's response as someone attempts to awake him from bed: "Just a little extra sleep, then I will get up." The young son is warned that habits of laziness and indulgence can quickly grow upon the best of people.

[34] So shall thy poverty come as one that travelleth; and thy want as an armed man.

The consequences of the lazy farmer's repeated actions and habits precipitate life-and-death consequences. The farmer finds himself financially destroyed because of his own laziness. A robber didn't steal all his money; his own sleep did.

Proverbs 25

[1] These are also proverbs of Solomon, which the men of Hezekiah king of Judah copied out.

The fourth collection of the book, chapters 25–29, took its form by means of scribes during the reign of Hezekiah in the 7th century. The proverbs of Solomon were likely memorized and orally transmitted for generations, but at the time of Hezekiah they were collected and then preserved in writing in one collection stored in the royal annals. Since peace and prosperity ensued for some of Hezekiah's reign, it was possible for art, literature, and religion to thrive in Israelite society.

[2] It is the glory of God to conceal a thing: but the honour of kings is to search out a matter.

Since God is a god "that hidest thyself" (Isaiah 45:15), it is agreeable with His nature that "the secret things belong" to Him (Deuteronomy 29:29) and that He keeps His reasoning for executing His will unknown. The king's duty is to discover that divine truth or reason and wisely apply it to his reign. Verses 2-7 are proverbs concerning kings.

[3] The heaven for height, and the earth for depth, and the heart of kings is unsearchable.

The divinely appointed descendent of David ruling over the nation of Israel has a glorious resemblance to God. Just as God's superior wisdom in creation made it impossible to reach the top of the heavens or the bottoms of the earth, so the king's unfathomable wisdom is unattainable to his subjects. As with God, this quality allows him to act as he pleases without explaining his reasoning.

[4] Take away the dross from the silver, and there shall come forth a vessel for the finer.

Verses 4-5 belong together. It was common knowledge that if the silversmith removed the impurities from silver through the process of refinement, the sterling would be ready for the smith to produce a vessel. Chaldean silver ornaments are known to exist from 2850 BC, some 700 years before the birth of Abraham.

[5] Take away the wicked from before the king, and his throne shall be established in righteousness.

Applying the maxim in the previous verse, if the king removes those wicked advisors from his court, as the silversmith removes the impurities from silver, his reign and dynasty are promised to remain secure through his pure and impartial execution of justice.

[6] Put not forth thyself in the presence of the king, and stand not in the place of great men:

Verses 5-6 belong together. The maxim is a warning to never break court etiquette by arrogantly intruding into the palace court and positioning yourself to petition the king or his counselors (Esther 5:2).

[7] For better it is that it be said unto thee, Come up hither; than that thou shouldest be put lower in the presence of the prince whom thine eyes have seen.

The application is that the promotion of the humble man is honorable, but the humbling of the proud man is shameful. This maxim is of course similar to the illustration used by Jesus of a wedding guest who tried to elbow their way to the front of the table and was shamefully removed (Luke 14:8-10).

[8] Go not forth hastily to strive, lest thou know not what to do in the end thereof, when thy neighbour hath put thee to shame.

The father warns the son against being quick to legal action because what would he do if his neighbor dealt him a shameful defeat in litigation? It's best to "leave off contention, before it be meddled with" (17:14).

[9] Debate thy cause with thy neighbour himself; and discover not a secret to another:

Verses 9-10 belong together. When arguing with your neighbor—or perhaps it means if you take your neighbor to court—don't unnecessarily involve others in the case by disclosing their secrets in order to help you win.

[10] Lest he that heareth it put thee to shame, and thine infamy turn not away.

The reason not to namedrop when making a deposition is because others may accuse you of gossip, and you will never regain your good reputation. The best advice is to "go and tell him his fault between thee and him alone" (Matthew 18:15).

[11] A word fitly spoken is like apples of gold in pictures of silver.

Timely advice is lovely and refreshing; it is comparable to the finest of summer fruits perfectly ripe with just the right color. Such sound advice would not be complete without being presented in the right way, in the finest of silver baskets.

[12] As an earring of gold, and an ornament of fine gold, so is a wise reprover upon an obedient ear.

Finishing the theme of taking sound advice from the wise, "a word fitly spoken" or valid criticism is as valuable and attractive to the recipient as a beautiful woman wearing golden jewelry.

[13] As the cold of snow in the time of harvest, so is a faithful messenger to them that send him: for he refresheth the soul of his masters.

It was apparently a luxurious custom to apply snow or ice to refresh a drink. It is possible Solomon would have experienced this practice in his Lebanese palace (1 Kings 9:19). The refreshing sensation of drinking an iced beverage in the heat of the day in May or June during harvest season is comparable to the peace of mind a faithful messenger gives to his master.

[14] Whoso boasteth himself of a false gift is like clouds and wind without rain.

A person who is full of hot air, who promises what they are going to do but doesn't produce, is comparable to the greatest disappointment of a farmer in the world of the Bible—dark rain clouds and wind (1 Kings 18:45), normally the precursor to heavy rains, that produce no precipitation.

[15] By long forbearing is a prince persuaded, and a soft tongue breaketh the bone.

Being poised and calm can cause the *qatsiyn*, or ruler, to be persuaded to the petitioner's cause, which is another way of saying that soft, not hard, speech can overcome the greatest obstacles.

[16] Hast thou found honey? eat so much as is sufficient for thee, lest thou be filled therewith, and vomit it.

To find honey in the world of the Bible was not an uncommon occurrence. Wild honey was normally located in hard-to-reach places like rock crevices and trees (1 Samuel 14:26). So, the father warns the son to eat in moderation, lest he have his fill of it and what was once sweet now becomes revolting.

[17] Withdraw thy foot from thy neighbour's house; lest he be weary of thee, and so hate thee.

Just as too much honey is not good for the young man, so too many visits to his friend's house is detrimental, making his friend sick of him.

Too much of anything, regardless of how sweet it may be, can bring contempt.

[18] A man that beareth false witness against his neighbour is a maul, and a sword, and a sharp arrow.

Telling lies about someone is just as cruel and harmful as hitting them with a mace (a rod with a ball of limestone on the end to be used as a club), wounding them with a sword, or shooting them with a sharp arrow, but lies take less courage than a physical confrontation.

[19] Confidence in an unfaithful man in time of trouble is like a broken tooth, and a foot out of joint.

Since it is vital to depend on the right people, the son is advised that an unreliable person cannot be trusted anytime, much less in a time of trouble, to accomplish the most basic of tasks like chewing or walking.

[20] As he that taketh away a garment in cold weather, and as vinegar upon nitre, so is he that singeth songs to an heavy heart.

When you see your friend has a heavy heart, mourn with them and comfort them instead of singing cheerful songs (Job 2:13). Being insensitive to a friend's feelings is compared to painful and unimaginable experiences of cruelty.

[21] If thine enemy be hungry, give him bread to eat; and if he be thirsty, give him water to drink:

Verses 21-22 belong together. Contrary to the likely predominant xenophobic view of "loving your neighbor but hating your enemy" (Matthew 5:43), the father advises the son that mercy triumphs over judgment.

[22] For thou shalt heap coals of fire upon his head, and the LORD shall reward thee.

Unexpected kindness—giving your enemy food to eat and water to drink—shames them, searing into their mind a moral lesson that violence could never accomplish. Such acts of generosity disarm an adversary, which is likely the reward of YHWH.

[23] The north wind driveth away rain: so doth an angry countenance a backbiting tongue.

Storm systems in the Holy Land normally come from the west or the southwest (Job 37:22, Luke 12:54) and are driven away by a strong north wind. In like manner, an angry look can drive away someone's evil speech.

[24] It is better to dwell in the corner of the housetop, than with a brawling woman and in a wide house.

It is recommended to live on a corner of the roof rather than to share a dry and comfortable luxurious house with a quarrelsome wife and make a bad situation worse. It was certainly plausible in antiquity to live on a roof (1 Samuel 9:26), though you could be exposed to inclement weather.

[25] As cold waters to a thirsty soul, so is good news from a far country.

It revives the soul (Genesis 45:27) to receive good news from a far country like Jacob did: "Joseph is yet alive, and he is the governor over all the land of Egypt" (Genesis 45:26). It is like a cup of cold water to a thirsty traveler.

[26] A righteous man falling down before the wicked is as a troubled fountain, and a corrupt spring.

If the godly man caves in to the peer pressure of the wicked, he is as useless to his righteous cause and as dangerous to the fabric of his society as a poisoned water fountain or a muddied spring.

[27] It is not good to eat much honey: so for men to search their own glory is not glory.

Eating too much honey can be harmful just as too much studying can be harmful, as in attempting to search out the secret things that belong only to the Lord our God (Deuteronomy 29:29).

[28] He that hath no rule over his own spirit is like a city that is broken down, and without walls.

A person with self-control is like "a city that is walled and very great" (Numbers 13:28) that can ward off anyone or anything that would be detrimental; but a person without self-control is described with the most vulnerable imagery in antiquity: a city with broken-down walls (2 Kings 25:10).

PROVERBS 26

[1] As snow in summer, and as rain in harvest, so honour is not seemly for a fool.

As unusual as it is for snow to fall in summertime, and as catastrophic as it is for heavy rain to fall in late springtime when the crops are ripe for harvest (1 Samuel 12:17), it is just as ridiculous to associate honor with a simpleton.

[2] As the bird by wandering, as the swallow by flying, so the curse causeless shall not come.

Like a fluttering sparrow that goes from place to place to avoid the hunter or a darting swallow that is impossible to trap, so in like manner an innocent person will escape the ensnarement of an undeserved curse.

[3] A whip for the horse, a bridle for the ass, and a rod for the fool's back.

As you would guide or sharply correct a horse with a whip and a donkey with a bridle, you correct the behavior of a simpleton not with words but by beating them with a thin tree limb or bush stock.

[4] Answer not a fool according to his folly, lest thou also be like unto him.

Verses 4-5 are a paradox and belong together. No matter what you say, you will never convert a fool from the error of their ways. By not answering their foolish questions, you won't run the risk of yourself being made a fool.

[5] Answer a fool according to his folly, lest he be wise in his own conceit.

Creating a paradox with the previous verse, the father warns the son not to allow the ramblings of a foolish man to go unchecked but to answer his questions in order to prevent him from thinking he is wiser than the wise man is.

[6] He that sendeth a message by the hand of a fool cutteth off the feet, and drinketh damage.

In the world of the Bible, a messenger would function as a bearer of news (Job 1:14), a bringer of requests (Numbers 20:14), a spy (Joshua 6:17), a deputy (2 Kings 5:10), or an envoy (2 Samuel 2:5). To send a fool to do a wise man's work could have disastrous consequences, thus the comparison to self-mutilation and drinking poison.

[7] The legs of the lame are not equal: so is a parable in the mouth of fools.

"Parable" and "proverb" are the same work. The word "proverb" comes from a Hebrew root meaning "to be like" or "to represent," which is fitting since many proverbs use comparisons to teach their truths. The English word "proverb" comes from the transliteration of the Latin *proverbia*. A brief expression of a generally recognized truth in the mouth of a fool is as useless as a paralyzed leg.

[8] As he that bindeth a stone in a sling, so is he that giveth honour to a fool.

As a stone bound in a slingshot is soon fired and to be found no more, so honor quickly departs from the presence of a fool. Or perhaps the sense is that using a precious stone in a sling where a fieldstone would be sufficient is as foolish as giving honor to a fool.

[9] As a thorn goeth up into the hand of a drunkard, so is a parable in the mouth of fools.

A fool who spouts off the sayings of the wise is as dangerous as a thorny branch brandished by a drunk since they don't know how to properly handle it and will only harm themselves and others.

[10] The great God that formed all things both rewardeth the fool, and rewardeth transgressors.

Though the Hebrew of this verse is difficult, it has nothing to do with the sense given in this translation. The idea of the maxim is an employer who indiscriminately hires any fool or passerby as a day laborer is as careless as an archer who shoots arrows at random.

[11] As a dog returneth to his vomit, so a fool returneth to his folly.

Eating its own vomit since it still contains the scent of food is that a normal function for an unclean dog; this was also how it was fed in part by its mother as a puppy. In the same way, a foolish man always returns to his disgusting habits.

[12] Seest thou a man wise in his own conceit? there is more hope of a fool than of him.

This Hebrew word for fool, *kesiluth*, indicates someone who is ignorant (Ecclesiastes 2:14), thoughtless (10:23), contentious (18:6), and lazy (Ecclesiastes 4:5). They disregard moral ideals and are a victim of their own stupidity. Yet, there is more hope for one of these *kesiluth* than for those "who are wise in their own eyes and prudent in their own sight" (Isaiah 5:21).

[13] The slothful man saith, There is a lion in the way; a lion is in the streets.

For a lazy person, no excuse is beyond the realm of possibility, no matter how remote it may be. The risk of being eaten by a lion in the streets is a good enough excuse for them to avoid the rigors of hard work. Verses 13-16 are a grouping about the lazy person.

[14] As the door turneth upon his hinges, so doth the slothful upon his bed.

Ancient doors usually were made of wood. Sometimes they were sheeted with metal for ornamentation (Isaiah 54:12) and defensive purposes, as in the case of city gates. Hinges, like we use now, were unknown in antiquity. Instead, doors turned on pivots set in sockets above and below. Like a door, the lazy person turns over in bed without any ambition to arise and work.

[15] The slothful hideth his hand in his bosom; it grieveth him to bring it again to his mouth.

In the ANE, diners would eat with their hands from a common dish set in the middle of table. Perhaps using a hyperbolic expression, lazy people will take the food in their hand (Matthew 26:23) but are so lazy they will not even do the necessary work to feed themselves.

[16] The sluggard is wiser in his own conceit than seven men that can render a reason.

The sluggard, who has the most ridiculous excuses to avoid work (26:13), is addicted to sleep (26:14). If he has food, he's so lazy that he wouldn't lift it to his mouth (26:15). And yet he still considers his private daydreams wiser than the perfect counsel of seven wise men.

[17] He that passeth by, and meddleth with strife belonging not to him, is like one that taketh a dog by the ears.

Interfering in someone else's argument is foolish and dangerous. The reward for not minding your own business is equivalent to the reward for grabbing a stray dog by the ears or tail (LXX). Wild dogs were vicious and renowned for their insatiable thirst for violence (2 Kings 9:35).

[18] As a mad man who casteth firebrands, arrows, and death,

Verses 18-19 belong together. The comparison begins with a madman who recklessly shoots arrows. The bow was an instrument employed early by Semites, showing up in a 1900 BC tomb painting at Beni-hasan in Egypt. Their bow is a well-developed weapon with a curved spring in it and attached string. The arrows were made of wood with metal heads and, as mentioned in this verse, occasionally augmented with a flammable material (Ephesians 6:16).

[19] So is the man that deceiveth his neighbour, and saith, Am not I in sport?

A mad man who carelessly shoots firebrand and arrows into the air is equated with someone who lies to their friends and then says, "I was just kidding."

[20] Where no wood is, there the fire goeth out: so where there is no talebearer, the strife ceaseth.

As a fire dies when you take away the fuel of wood, in like manner quarreling disappears when you take away the fuel of gossipers from your circle of companions. You can't have one without the other.

[21] As coals are to burning coals, and wood to fire; so is a contentious man to kindle strife.

The analogy—a quarrelsome person starts fights as easily as hot embers light charcoal or fire lights wood—was taken from daily life. Many types of ovens were built in the world of the Bible, from clay ovens set into interior wall corners, to interior open hearths with a center smoke hole (Hosea 13:3), to outdoor ovens built with the lower opening positioned to take advantage of the prevailing winds.

[22] The words of a talebearer are as wounds, and they go down into the innermost parts of the belly.

This is a poor translation. Rumors are not like "wounds" but are "gulped or swallowed down" like the choicest desserts; that is to say, they are quickly and irresistibly consumed, treasured up in the inmost part of the false accuser.

[23] Burning lips and a wicked heart are like a potsherd covered with silver dross.

The hypocrisy of smooth words may disguise a clever and wicked heart, just as a smooth glazing covered an earthen clay pottery vessel.

This glazing was likely a shiny metallic oxide with lead used as a pigment. Verses 23-26 are a grouping on hypocrisy.

[24] He that hateth dissembleth with his lips, and layeth up deceit within him;

Saying the same thing as the previous maxim but in a different way, the father advises his son that hateful people may cover-speak pleasant words, but beware because they're deceiving you.

[25] When he speaketh fair, believe him not: for there are seven abominations in his heart.

Hypocrites pretend to be kind, but don't believe them because their hearts are replete with evil. A real-life example of this parable would be Joab taking Abner "aside in the gate," a dark corner in the vaulted gateway where they might retire and converse unseen, and then he murdered Abner (2 Samuel 3:27).

[26] Whose hatred is covered by deceit, his wickedness shall be shewed before the whole congregation.

Finishing the grouping on hypocrisy, while a hypocrite's hatred may be concealed by trickery, the true intents and thoughts of their heart will eventually be unmasked, causing people to see through their lies.

[27] Whoso diggeth a pit shall fall therein: and he that rolleth a stone, it will return upon him.

The just retribution of YHWH is displayed when a devious man sets a trap for others and ends up getting caught in it himself. Much the same way, a soldier rolls a large stone up a height in order to hurl it down upon the enemy, but it ends up rolling back upon him.

[28] A lying tongue hateth those that are afflicted by it; and a flattering mouth worketh ruin.

The theme of evil speech which has dominated the last ten verses ends here. Serving as a final warning, the father warns the son of the destructive nature of an evil tongue which brings hurt and ruin upon its victims.

PROVERBS 27

[1] Boast not thyself of tomorrow; for thou knowest not what a day may bring forth.

This maxim, echoed in other Bible passages (Matthew 6:34, James 4:13), advises the son not to take life for granted since many of the events in the course of our daily lives are out of our control.

[2] Let another man praise thee, and not thine own mouth; a stranger, and not thine own lips.

Continuing the theme of advising against boasting, the father warns the son not to brag about his personal accomplishments, which would be the sin of pride (6:17), but to instead let someone else compliment him.

[3] A stone is heavy, and the sand weighty; but a fool's wrath is heavier than them both.

It is common knowledge that a stone is heavy and sand is weighty (Job 6:3), but what the young son may not know is that the resentment caused by a fool is figurately heavier and harder to bear than any load of stone or sand could ever be (Sirach 22:15).

[4] Wrath is cruel, and anger is outrageous; but who is able to stand before envy?

Using the same structure as the previous maxim, the father warns the son that a man filled with wrath can be punishing and a furious man overwhelming, but a jealous man is "heavier than them both" and the most dangerous of them all.

[5] Open rebuke is better than secret love.

In another "better than" proverb, the father advises the son that if he really loves his friend or family member, he should take the courage to "tell him his fault between thee and him alone" (Matthew 18:15).

[6] Faithful are the wounds of a friend; but the kisses of an enemy are deceitful.

Finishing the pairing of the previous proverb, the wounds of a friend, being equivalent to open rebuke, are to be preferred over the numerous kisses from an enemy who hides his hatred (Matthew 26:49). To kiss another's cheek, beard, hands, or feet was the greatest token of affection, greeting, or reverence in antiquity.

[7] The full soul loatheth an honeycomb; but to the hungry soul every bitter thing is sweet.

Perhaps the sense of the maxim is to show the "disadvantage" that often accompanies having an abundance and the "advantage" of the destitute so that the wealthy wise man may learn to be moderate and the poor wise man may learn to be satisfied.

[8] As a bird that wandereth from her nest, so is a man that wandereth from his place.

A person who strays from their land and family is a stranger in a strange land and vulnerable to the customs and mannerisms of the land they are visiting. This maxim is typified in the narrative of the sojourning of Abraham. Ideally, a man wants to live out his days and "die in [his] nest" (Job 29:18).

[9] Ointment and perfume rejoice the heart: so doth the sweetness of a man's friend by hearty counsel.

The heartfelt counsel of a wise friend is as sweet and rare as perfume and incense. Perfume and incense were luxurious commodities that were often imported to ancient Israel. Cinnamon was found on the coast of India and was converted into incense and perfume. Frankincense was found in Oman and Yemen and was listed as one of the treasures of the Temple in Jerusalem. Incense was produced from this gum resin, and it was also used to stop bleeding. Myrrh was found in Arabia, Ethiopia, and Somalia. Incense and aromatic oils were produced from this gum resin. Myrrh was also used for medicinal purposes as a pain reliever. In Egypt, myrrh was used for embalming. And pepper, found in India, was used mainly as seasoning.

[10] Thine own friend, and thy father's friend, forsake not; neither go into thy brother's house in the day of thy calamity: for better is a neighbour that is near than a brother far off.

The father advises the son not to rely only on the blood relations within his clan or tribe because his kinsman may live too far away to help in a timely manner, but instead to also rely on his nearby friend or a family friend even though there is no blood tie.

[11] My son, be wise, and make my heart glad, that I may answer him that reproacheth me.

Again, the chief literary device of the book is that of a father speaking to a son, thus reinforcing an ideology, the code of the family. If the son or student did not show wisdom, if he forsook the teaching of his parents, the father (teacher) would bear the shame and be blamed for the failure of his son's education.

[12] A prudent man foreseeth the evil, and hideth himself; but the simple pass on, and are punished.

There are numerous examples of the wise foreseeing imminent danger and taking the necessary precautions: Noah, Lot, the Israelites during the plagues of Egypt. In contrast, the simpleton goes blindly on and suffers the deadly consequences.

[13] Take his garment that is surety for a stranger, and take a pledge of him for a strange woman.

The proverb is probably more advice to moneylenders than condemnation for cosigners (6:1-5). Wise creditors should require collateral, such as the garment for those foolhardy enough to cosign a debt for a stranger (Exodus 22:26).

[14] He that blesseth his friend with a loud voice, rising early in the morning, it shall be counted a curse to him.

There is a time and place for everything, so don't salute your neighbor with a loud and cheerful greeting too early in the morning. As he awakens from his deep sleep, this ostentatious greeting will be received as no blessing but a curse.

[15] A continual dropping in a very rainy day and a contentious woman are alike.

Verses 15-16 belong together. A nagging wife who wears out the patience of her husband is as detrimental and unstoppable as a leaky roof. Roofs in the world of the Bible were mostly flat and were accessible by exterior stairs. Roofs were usually formed of clay packed with stone rollers, supported by mats of rushes or branches across wood beams or palm tree trunks (Mark 2:4).

[16] Whosoever hideth her hideth the wind, and the ointment of his right hand, which bewrayeth itself.

Stopping the complaints of a nagging wife is impossible. It's compared to trying to stop the wind, and if he puts out his hand to try and stop her, she slips right through as if his hands were greased with oil. So, remove yourself from her company until her wrath subsides (21:9).

[17] Iron sharpeneth iron; so a man sharpeneth the countenance of his friend.

The ancient Israelites had an abundance of the natural resources in Israel (Deuteronomy 8:9). But the secret of toughening the metal by repeated hammering when hot, "iron sharpening iron," and its subsequent quenching with water was apparently guarded by the Hittites and later made known to the Israelites through trade ties with the Phoenicians and Philistines. The countenance, mind, or heart is mutually affected by those with whom we keep company.

[18] Whoso keepeth the fig tree shall eat the fruit thereof: so he that waiteth on his master shall be honoured.

As workers who tend a fig tree year after year are allowed to eat the fruit of their reward at harvest, and as servants who protect their master's interests will be rewarded (Matthew 25:21), so anything the young man works hard at is bound to produce results.

[19] As in water face answereth to face, so the heart of man to man.

As reflections are accurate portrayals of what is being represented, so the heart (the inner control center of the person and the portion of man of which God is most concerned; 1 Samuel 16:7) produces actions that correspond to the quality of the heart.

[20] Hell and destruction are never full; so the eyes of man are never satisfied.

To the ancients, hell or *sheol* was a subterranean place full of thick darkness (Job 10:21) where the dead abode. The underworld is depicted as having valleys or depths (9:18) and a city with walls (Jonah 2:6) and gates (Isaiah 38:10). The word *sheol* is derived from the idea of asking or demanding; it is a place that is never full. On average 240,000 people die daily, 10,000 every hour and 167 a minute. Just as hell is never full, neither is human desire.

[21] As the fining pot for silver, and the furnace for gold; so is a man to his praise.

As a blacksmith heats a crucible to refine and purify silver and a furnace for gold (Malachi 3:3), so that quality or attribute on which a man prides or praises himself on proves what sort of man he truly is.

[22] Though thou shouldest bray a fool in a mortar among wheat with a pestle, yet will not his foolishness depart from him.

Grinding is a procedure by which grain is reduced to flour through being pulverized between an upper and lower millstone (Matthew 24:41). This example from daily life is used to illustrate that fools are so stubborn that even if they are proverbially ground to dust, they will not let go of their precious, foolish choices.

[23] Be thou diligent to know the state of thy flocks, and look well to thy herds.

Verses 23-24 belong together. Wealth in the world of the Bible was measured through precious metals and clothing (James 5:2-3), as well as land, servants, livestock, etc. The father advises the son to know the "state" or number (LXX) of his possessions so he may preserve and improve upon his wealth. Verses 23-27 praise the slow-paced, conservative, and tight-knit lifestyle of pastoral life.

[24] For riches are not for ever: and doth the crown endure to every generation?

The reason the son is to know well the financial state of his family's ANE portfolio is because if he doesn't manage it correctly, it will not last. Just as if a man had the wealth of a kingdom but did not maintain and manage it with diligence, it would disappear. It is no surprise the greatest Israelite kings minded shepherding and husbandry.

[25] The hay appeareth, and the tender grass sheweth itself, and herbs of the mountains are gathered.

Verses 25-27 belong together. Just as the livestock must be made the most of, so too the fields must be maximized to their greatest potential. This was done by staggering plantings so different crops could be harvested at different times of year, as well as rotating crops to get the greatest yield.

[26] The lambs are for thy clothing, and the goats are the price of the field.

The investment of the crop wisely managed and harvested will provide the wise farmer with the dividend of food for the sheep and goats, which in turn will provide the commodities of wool from the sheep, milk from the goats, and money from goats sold.

[27] And thou shalt have goats' milk enough for thy food, for the food of thy household, and for the maintenance for thy maidens.

The young son is advised by his father's past experiences that wisdom and hard work are necessary to properly managing and taking full advantage of his family's assets in order to preserve and improve them for the next generation.

PROVERBS 28

[1] The wicked flee when no man pursueth: but the righteous are bold as a lion.

The cursed condition of the nation of Israel during their chastisement is depicted in the Torah (Leviticus 26:17) with this same language: "running away when no one is chasing them." In their blessed condition, Israel was like the godly ones in this verse, being so bold that five of them could chase a hundred (Leviticus 26:8).

[2] For the transgression of a land many are the princes thereof: but by a man of understanding and knowledge the state thereof shall be prolonged.

When there is moral rot within a nation, its government topples easily. This is perfectly illustrated in the history of the northern kingdom of Israel, especially in the disastrous period of rule after the death of Jeroboam II up to the Assyrian deportation. Conversely, in the history of the southern kingdom of Judah, wise and knowledgeable leaders often brought stability.

[3] A poor man that oppresseth the poor is like a sweeping rain which leaveth no food.

The most unthinkable and catastrophic occurrence that could happen to the ancient agriculturally based Israelite community is for YHWH to send thunder and rain at the grain harvest (1 Samuel 12:17). So is the wickedness of a "ruler," "poor man," or "evil man" (the Hebrew is unclear) that destroys the only profitable possession of a poor man.

[4] They that forsake the law praise the wicked: but such as keep the law contend with them.

To reject the Torah (instruction), which was a promise of security when obeyed and properly implemented, is to follow the ways of the wicked. But those who obey the Torah are filled with righteous indignation when they see the law of God made ineffective by the wicked and desire to "contend with them" or have justice prevail.

[5] Evil men understand not judgment: but they that seek the LORD understand all things.

The evil or natural person doesn't understand biblical justice. It is foolishness to him; neither can he know it because these things are spiritually discerned, but those who follow YHWH can evaluate and make judgment on all things.

[6] Better is the poor that walketh in his uprightness, than he that is perverse in his ways, though he be rich.

The contrast in this maxim is between the two general classes of society: the haves and the have nots. The twist in this verse is that "the haves" are the poor but honest men and "the have nots" are the rich but dishonest men. Honesty is the best policy even if it results in poverty.

[7] Whoso keepeth the law is a wise son: but he that is a companion of riotous men shameth his father.

The son must choose between those values that preserve society (the code of his family) and alternative actions (riotous living) that undercut family stability. Acknowledging the shame associated with such licentious living, the Torah permitted capital punishment for such rebellious children (Deuteronomy 21:20-21).

[8] He that by usury and unjust gain increaseth his substance, he shall gather it for him that will pity the poor.

The unjust person whose income comes from charging high interest rates (Exodus 22:25) will end up having his money taken from him and redistributed to someone else (Luke 19:24), someone who is kind to the poor.

[9] He that turneth away his ear from hearing the law, even his prayer shall be abomination.

The maxim reprimands those who thought they found favor with YHWH by their numerous and lengthy prayers (Matthew 6:5) despite their disobedience to the spirit of the Torah. If we do not listen to God, He will not listen to us when we pray.

[10] Whoso causeth the righteous to go astray in an evil way, he shall fall himself into his own pit: but the upright shall have good things in possession.

Continuing the theme of reprisal in verses 8-9, the just retribution of YHWH is displayed when a devious man sets a trap for the righteous but ends up getting caught in it himself. The upright or blameless, by contrast, are not punished but blessed with long life and an inheritance.

[11] The rich man is wise in his own conceit; but the poor that hath understanding searcheth him out.

Rich people may think they are wise, that their wealth is representative of their wisdom, but wisdom cannot be bought with money. A poor person with discernment knows the rich person better than they know themselves since they can see right through their façade.

[12] When righteous men do rejoice, there is great glory: but when the wicked rise, a man is hidden.

When the godly ruling class succeeds, everyone is glad. When the political system is corrupted, those who are wise stay under the radar because of the power and depravity of the ruling class (Amos 5:13).

[13] He that covereth his sins shall not prosper: but whoso confesseth and forsaketh them shall have mercy.

Contrary to popular belief, the proud are not blessed, and evildoers do not prosper (Malachi 3:15). People who conceal their sins, exemplified first in Adam (Genesis 3:8), deceive themselves and will not succeed; but if they confess their sins, God is faithful and just to forgive them of their sins (1 John 1:9).

[14] Happy is the man that feareth alway: but he that hardeneth his heart shall fall into mischief.

A blessing is bestowed upon those who fear to do wrong, to sin against YHWH, who keep the teacher's basic theme and motto of the book, a reverential fear of YHWH. But the stubborn, on the other hand, who do not fear YHWH are headed for serious trouble. Everything one does proves or disproves their relationship with or fear of YHWH.

[15] As a roaring lion, and a ranging bear; so is a wicked ruler over the poor people.

Encounters with lions and bears were apparently not all too uncommon in antiquity (1 Kings 13:24, 2 Kings 2:24). The fierce attributes and characteristics of these wild animals are compared to the fury of an ANE ruler. To rouse his anger is to risk having him devour you.

[16] The prince that wanteth understanding is also a great oppressor: but he that hateth covetousness shall prolong his days.

A ruler with no wisdom oppresses his subjects. This is typified in the last king of Judah, Jehoiakim, who built his palace with forced labor and infused injustice into its walls (Jeremiah 22:13). But the effect of a ruler who hates corruption is the promise of a long reign, typified in David (1 Kings 2:11).

[17] A man that doeth violence to the blood of any person shall flee to the pit; let no man stay him.

A murderer will be a fugitive until death. For the deliberate murderer, there was no city of refuge to take protection in from the vengeance of the family of the person he has slain. The father commands his son to not aid or abet a deliberate murderer.

[18] Whoso walketh uprightly shall be saved: but he that is perverse in his ways shall fall at once.

The contrast in this maxim is between the two general classes of the book of Proverbs, the wise and the foolish. Those who are blameless will be rescued from harm, but those who are "crooked in two ways," or two-faced, will eventually have their other side catch up with them.

[19] He that tilleth his land shall have plenty of bread: but he that followeth after vain persons shall have poverty enough.

In a contrast between industry and idleness, the wise farmer who spends his time tilling the land will produce a sure return, but the foolish farmer who neglects his business will be reduced to poverty and moral depravity.

[20] A faithful man shall abound with blessings: but he that maketh haste to be rich shall not be innocent.

The wise man who manages his hard-earned money watches it grow slowly but surely over time, whereas undeserved money gotten by a get-rich-quick scheme like gambling or high-interest usury has a tendency to get the unwise man into trouble.

[21] To have respect of persons is not good: for for a piece of bread that man will transgress.

In regard to the administration of justice, it is evil to judge someone based on appearance rather than merit. Discernment is needed in judgment because some people can be persuaded to compromise justice for the smallest price, a piece of bread.

[22] He that hasteth to be rich hath an evil eye, and considereth not that poverty shall come upon him.

The hazard here is the greed of a covetous person who, to quickly amass wealth, will make use of any means necessary, even immoral means such as gambling. This lust to get rich quick causes others to defraud him, and in the end assigns him to abject poverty.

[23] He that rebuketh a man afterwards shall find more favour than he that flattereth with the tongue.

In the end, people who wander from the truth appreciate honest criticism far more than flattery since it converts them from the error of their ways, saving their soul from death and covering a multitude of sins (James 5:19).

[24] Whoso robbeth his father or his mother, and saith, It is no transgression; the same is the companion of a destroyer.

The son faces a choice of allegiance, whether to contribute to a godly society or to join the ranks of society's dissidents. The son who steals from his parents and says, "What's wrong with that?" has chosen the company of dissidents and destroys the fabric of his society.

[25] He that is of a proud heart stirreth up strife: but he that putteth his trust in the LORD shall be made fat.

Just as impatience (15:18), gossip (16:28), and a contentious spirit (26:21) stir up conflict, so does greed. Opposed to the covetous are the patient who trust in YHWH to be "made fat" or become greatly blessed in material things.

[26] He that trusteth in his own heart is a fool: but whoso walketh wisely, he shall be delivered.

The arrogant one or *keciyl* is self-sufficient and trusts in his own heart, which is desperately wicked (Jeremiah 17:9), in his quest for wisdom. This is opposed to the man who "trusts in YHWH with all his heart" (3:5) to help him attain wisdom.

[27] He that giveth unto the poor shall not lack: but he that hideth his eyes shall have many a curse.

The wise person who gives their money liberally to those in need becomes even more blessed (Matthew 6:3-4), whereas the stingy person who hides their eyes from the beggar (Isaiah 1:15) ends up being cursed themselves with poverty (Sirach 4:5).

[28] When the wicked rise, men hide themselves: but when they perish, the righteous increase.

When the government is administered by wicked rulers like King Amon of Judah (2 Kings 21:21), those who are wise stay under the radar because of the depravity of the ruling class (Amos 5:13). But when the next generation is a godly ruling class, like Amon's son Josiah, the righteous take back control of the government and the nation thrives.

PROVERBS 29

[1] He, that being often reproved hardeneth his neck, shall suddenly be destroyed, and that without remedy.

If the son doesn't take the advice of his father and instead hardens his neck, a metaphor taken from a stubborn, noncompliant ox, and refuses to accept the yoke of criticism, he will suddenly be "destroyed" or shattered to pieces like a potter's vessel beyond recovery (Psalm 2:9).

[2] When the righteous are in authority, the people rejoice: but when the wicked beareth rule, the people mourn.

As in the days of King David (1 Chronicles 29:9), the subjects of a monarch rejoice when a ruler is a man after God's own heart (1 Samuel 13:14); this is opposed to the reign of a wicked ruler typified in Manasseh (2 Chronicles 33:2), when the subjects suffer violence and injustice.

[3] Whoso loveth wisdom rejoiceth his father: but he that keepeth company with harlots spendeth his substance.

The son faces a choice of allegiance, whether to contribute to a godly society by obeying his father and teacher (Ephesians 6:1), or to join the ranks of society's dissidents by hiring prostitutes, squandering his wealth, and bringing great shame to his family (Luke 15:30).

[4] The king by judgment establisheth the land: but he that receiveth gifts overthroweth it.

A king—the fountainhead of all religious and political policies in antiquity—who is just and makes the right decisions gives stability to his nation, but an unjust king who "receives gifts," or sells justice through bribes, destroys the stability of his government.

[5] A man that flattereth his neighbour spreadeth a net for his feet.

Those who blindly flatter those closest to them by not being honest but instead tickling their ears bring them to death. Different translations portray either the flatterer or the friend as being ensnared in the trap of deceit.

[6] In the transgression of an evil man there is a snare: but the righteous doth sing and rejoice.

The wicked are entangled in problems by their self-incriminating speech; but even when the godly fall into a snare set by the wicked, their wise speech and behavior allow them to escape from trouble and shout for joy.

[7] The righteous considereth the cause of the poor: but the wicked regardeth not to know it.

The righteous, whether a king, judge, priest, or commoner, is not a respecter of persons based on social status; he is even concerned with justice for the lowest castes of society. But the wicked, on the other hand, will not waste his time with such compassion since it doesn't personally benefit him.

[8] Scornful men bring a city into a snare: but wise men turn away wrath.

Troublemakers can get a whole town agitated, or fan the flames of fire, through their destructive rebellion. But the wise will calm the anger of their neighbors through their wise council. This parable is typified in the account of the wise woman at Abel of Beth-maachah who suppressed the revolt of Sheba in her wisdom (2 Samuel 20:13-26).

[9] If a wise man contendeth with a foolish man, whether he rage or laugh, there is no rest.

If a wise person takes a fool to court, the teacher warns that there is no way to settle a lawsuit with the fool, to peacefully resolve the conflict, whether it be through vehement threats or logical persuasion.

[10] The bloodthirsty hate the upright: but the just seek his soul.

The blessed life of a man of integrity is a constant source of jealousy and hate to a bloodthirsty fool; but while men of bloodshed try to ruin the upright, the upright seeks to help them, to preserve their life. This proverb is typified in the account of David's mercy to Saul in the cave at Ein Gedi (1 Samuel 24:10).

[11] A fool uttereth all his mind: but a wise man keepeth it in till afterwards.

A fool "goes forth" or gives full vent to what is on his mind or heart. But the wise, even though they are angry, do not sin but quietly hold their anger back until it is the proper time to vent it before the sun goes down (Ephesians 4:26).

[12] If a ruler hearken to lies, all his servants are wicked.

If a ruler is willing to be deceived by hearing only what he wants to hear from his yes-men instead of unpleasant realities, as typified in the prophecy of Micaiah to Ahab (1 Kings 22:13-28), then all his advisers will enthusiastically provide him with deceitful counsel.

[13] The poor and the deceitful man meet together: the Lord lighteneth both their eyes.

The poor and their oppressor have nothing in common except one thing, that YHWH made them both, and in that one area they are equal. YHWH does not "regard the rich more than the poor. For they all are the work of his hands" (Job 34:19).

[14] The king that faithfully judgeth the poor, his throne shall be established for ever.

In the cause-and-effect world of the Bible, if the king is not a respecter of persons and judges the lowest and least-regarded class of society, the poor, fairly, then his dynasty is promised to be stable and to continue for many generations.

[15] The rod and reproof give wisdom: but a child left to himself bringeth his mother to shame.

To discipline a child through spanking them with the rod drives out folly and produces wisdom, but a parent who spares the rod ends up being publicly disgraced later in life by their intentionally undisciplined child. This parable is typified in the account of Absalom, whose "father had not displeased him at any time" (1 Kings 1:6); consequently, he lacked respect for authority and eventually sought to assassinate and supplant his father, King David.

[16] When the wicked are multiplied, transgression increaseth: but the righteous shall see their fall.

When the wicked are in authority of the religious and political systems, sin is condoned and naturally trickles down from the top; but the godly are comforted that divine retribution will overtake the wicked.

[17] Correct thy son, and he shall give thee rest; yea, he shall give delight unto thy soul.

A promise is given that if you discipline your children, which moves them from immaturity to maturity, they will give you, their parents, peace of mind and make your heart joyful as they walk in truth (3 John 1:4).

[18] Where there is no vision, the people perish: but he that keepeth the law, happy is he.

"Where there is no vision"—which does not mean a person's ability to create a goal but is synonymous with YHWH's guidance, revelation, and authority—people will cast off restraint as typified in the period of Eli the Priest (1 Samuel 3:1) and Asa the King (2 Chronicles 15:3).

On the other hand, blessed is the man whose delight is in the law of YHWH (Psalm 1:2).

[19] A servant will not be corrected by words: for though he understand he will not answer.

Words alone will not teach a servant what is required any more than they will teach a young child what is required. Though the words may be understood, they are not heeded (Luke 12:47). Therefore, the foolish servant can only be corrected by many stripes.

[20] Seest thou a man that is hasty in his words? there is more hope of a fool than of him.

This Hebrew word for fool, *kesiluth*, indicates someone who is ignorant (Ecclesiastes 2:14), thoughtless (10:23), contentious (18:6), and lazy (Ecclesiastes 4:5). They disregard moral ideals and are a victim of their own stupidity. Yet, there is more hope for a *kesiluth* than for those who speak without thinking.

[21] He that delicately bringeth up his servant from a child shall have him become his son at the length.

A servant undisciplined and pampered from childhood will bring grief to their master when they become a rebel. Servants are to be disciplined by their masters just as children are by their parents, lest they shame their master.

[22] An angry man stirreth up strife, and a furious man aboundeth in transgression.

In warning the son against losing control of his emotions, the father equates an angry person who lacks the fruit of patience and is quick to start fights with a hot-tempered man guilty of committing all kinds of sin.

[23] A man's pride shall bring him low: but honour shall uphold the humble in spirit.

The theme of this proverb is continually enforced throughout the book. Pride, the sin God hates most (6:16-17), is the underlying cause of men's humiliation. But the antithesis of this, a man who hates pride, will be exalted (Luke 14:11).

[24] Whoso is partner with a thief hateth his own soul: he heareth cursing, and bewrayeth it not.

If you assist a thief, you will only hurt himself. For when you are caught and brought before the judge and sworn to tell the truth, you dare not testify against your "friends" for fear of retaliation. The young man ends up committing perjury and compounding his crime (Leviticus 5:1).

[25] The fear of man bringeth a snare: but whoso putteth his trust in the LORD shall be safe.

In the face of fierce opposition, the son is not to fear those who can kill the body but are unable to kill the soul. Instead, he is to place his confidence in YHWH, who keeps him safe—literally he shall be "set on high" above the threatening danger below.

[26] Many seek the ruler's favour; but every man's judgment cometh from the LORD.

Many will curry the favor of a public official, often through bribes, in the hopes of receiving justice or some favor from them; but the son is advised not to follow the course of the many but to understand that ultimately justice comes from YHWH.

[27] An unjust man is an abomination to the just: and he that is upright in the way is abomination to the wicked.

Since this is the last maxim of Solomon, it is fitting that he ends with this great moral contrast: the righteous despise the unjust, just as the wicked despise the godly. The world chooses one side or the other, wisdom or folly, and the choices we make are the evidence of which side we have chosen.

Proverbs 30

[1] The words of Agur the son of Jakeh, even the prophecy: the man spake unto Ithiel, even unto Ithiel and Ucal,

The sayings of Agur son of Jakeh begin with a somber tone. The second half of this verse could be better translated "I am weary, O God; I am weary and worn out, O God." Some understand this section (30:1-14) as Agur being a skeptic and challenging traditional wisdom. If this is the case, a speaker starting in 30:5 rebukes Agur for unorthodoxy and warns him against adding to the teacher's words.

[2] Surely I am more brutish than any man, and have not the understanding of a man.

Verses 2-3 continue the *massa* or weighty oracle in the previous verse, that the heavy hand of God is on Agur. He continues by stating that he is a natural brute beast and is totally incompetent in understanding the subject matter of the book of Proverbs because it is spiritually discerned.

[3] I neither learned wisdom, nor have the knowledge of the holy.

Agur continues his confession by stating that he is ignorant and unlearned, nor does he have any knowledge of the holy, which is the teacher's basic theme and the motto of the book—namely, that the first step toward wisdom is having a reverential fear of YHWH (1:7).

[4] Who hath ascended up into heaven, or descended? who hath gathered the wind in his fists? who hath bound the waters in a garment? who hath established all the ends of the earth? what is his name, and what is his son's name, if thou canst tell?

The reason for the despondent spirit of Agur is revealed in this verse. Since the answers to his questions are above and beyond all human understanding, he demands that if anyone knows who can do these things, they must tell him.

[5] Every word of God is pure: he is a shield unto them that put their trust in him.

Verses 5-6 belong together. From the uncertainty of human speculation, a vertical view of life, Agur finds relief in a horizontal view of life, the perfection of divine revelation. Those who have a knowledge of God through His Word are afforded divine protection. This protection is compared to one of the most effective defensive "weapons" in antiquity, the shield. This word for shield is *magen,* a round-shaped shield that was smaller than the *sinna* shield. Shields were made of leather (2 Samuel 1:21) and of a wooden material that could be ornamented.

[6] Add thou not unto his words, lest he reprove thee, and thou be found a liar.

This verse is a threat of divine judgment in order to safeguard the integrity of the Word of God. The wording is a clear allusion to a threat mentioned twice in Deuteronomy regarding adding or taking away from the Torah: "Whatsoever thing I command you, observe to do it: thou shalt not add thereto, nor diminish from it" (Deuteronomy 4:2, 12:32) and later used by John in Revelation (Revelation 22:18).

[7] Two things have I required of thee; deny me them not before I die:

Verses 7-9 belong together. The rest of the oracle of Agur, verses

7-33, include several clusters of verses which are introduced by numbers. Agur begs for two favors from God while he is still alive that are revealed in the following verse.

[8] Remove far from me vanity and lies: give me neither poverty nor riches; feed me with food convenient for me:

Agur prays first for protection from deceit and lies, and then for God to meet his daily needs—and not necessarily meet his wants—with daily bread, somewhere between the extremities of poverty and riches.

[9] Lest I be full, and deny thee, and say, Who is the LORD? or lest I be poor, and steal, and take the name of my God in vain.

The reason for the petition is that great wealth has a tendency to make someone "deny" or become independent of YHWH to meet their physical needs, and poverty can lead to stealing, which finds fault with YHWH's provision. Either scenario dishonors the name of God whom the person claims to worship.

[10] Accuse not a servant unto his master, lest he curse thee, and thou be found guilty.

Agur advises the reader to mind their own business and never slander a servant or employee to their master or employer since the effect will be that the person you accused will curse you, and you will end up paying for it through some form of retribution.

[11] There is a generation that curseth their father, and doth not bless their mother.

Verses 11-31 contain six groups of four quaternions (sets of four people or things), each having a relation in language and thought. Verses 11-14 is the first quaternion and is a list of the most detestable people. First in line are children who dishonor their parents (Exodus 20:12).

[12] There is a generation that are pure in their own eyes, and yet is not washed from their filthiness.

The next group of detestable people are self-righteous hypocrites which are blinded to their own faults. This prevents them from receiving constructive criticism which could wash them from their "filthiness" or excrement.

[13] There is a generation, O how lofty are their eyes! and their eyelids are lifted up.

The next group of detestable people are proud persons whose "eyelids are lifted up." Pride has as its seat of emotion the heart, but it is often manifested and displayed on the face of man (Isaiah 10:12).

[14] There is a generation, whose teeth are as swords, and their jaw teeth as knives, to devour the poor from off the earth, and the needy from among men.

The last group of detestable people are people with incalculable greed. Their actions of extortion and usury against the poor are as deadly as swords and knives. They pride themselves on devouring those who cannot defend themselves.

[15] The horseleach hath two daughters, crying, Give, give. There are three things that are never satisfied, yea, four things say not, It is enough:

Verses 15-16 are the second quaternion and are a list of things that are unquenchable, using the example of a leech or literally a "sucking." The last clause of the verse is a Hebrew figure of speech used to emphasize their insatiable appetite.

[16] The grave; and the barren womb; the earth that is not filled with water; and the fire that saith not, It is enough.

The things that demand more than anyone can ever give are the grave (*sheol* is derived from the word for asking or demanding; it is a place that is never full, see 27:20), the desire of a woman's womb that is restrained from bearing a child (Genesis 16:2), the dry ground of Israel which can never get enough rain (Isaiah 53:2), and fire that devours everything it touches. Their desire feeds upon itself and produces a constant craving that can never be satisfied.

[17] The eye that mocketh at his father, and despiseth to obey his mother, the ravens of the valley shall pick it out, and the young eagles shall eat it.

The rebellious son that breaks the code of the family by deriding a father and despising a mother's instructions will not only die an early death but be dealt the horrible fate of not being buried with their family as their eyes are blinded by ravens and their rotting corpse is eaten by vultures (Revelation 19:17-18).

[18] There be three things which are too wonderful for me, yea, four which I know not:

Even though three would be a sufficient number, it is amplified by a fourth to accommodate the format and style of the author and to lead up to the crescendo of the illustration of things which leave no trace. Verses 18-20 are the third quaternion.

[19] The way of an eagle in the air; the way of a serpent upon a rock; the way of a ship in the midst of the sea; and the way of a man with a maid.

The mysterious workings of an eagle gliding through the sky, a snake slithering on a rock, a ship navigating in the ocean, and a man loving a virgin all venture into territory into which no one has ever gone before and leave no physical evidence of them ever being there.

[20] Such is the way of an adulterous woman; she eateth, and wipeth her mouth, and saith, I have done no wickedness.

The adulterous woman who after she sexually consumes a man, with the same conscience as she would consume a meal, states that there is no trace of her guilt, just as there is no trace of that which is wonderful in the previous verse.

[21] For three things the earth is disquieted, and for four which it cannot bear:

In the repetition of this strongly idiomatic phrase and literary device to represent a whole sum, the author begins the fourth quaternion in verses 21-23, which are a list of things which are inconceivable.

[22] For a servant when he reigneth; and a fool when he is filled with meat;

The first two things which are inconceivable because of the high level of incompatibility are a slave who would become king and a *nabal* or wicked person who is wise enough to prosper and be satisfied.

[23] For an odious woman when she is married; and an handmaid that is heir to her mistress.

The last two things which are inconceivable are a bitter woman who finally gets a husband and a servant girl who supplants her mistress. The sense of this quaternion is that it is not natural that an inferior should supplant a superior. For a society to flourish, each member must know their place, so it is best that the natural order of things be left undisturbed.

[24] There be four things which are little upon the earth, but they are exceeding wise:

In another repetition of grouping four things together, although the phrasing is slightly different from the others, the author begins the fifth quaternion in verses 24-28, which are a list of things whose amount of wisdom exceeds their naturally small size.

[25] The ants are a people not strong, yet they prepare their meat in the summer;

The author asks us to take a lesson from ants considering work ethic, to watch how hard they work, how heavy their loads are, and how they always seem to be active. Since ants are totally independent creatures having no overseer to make them work, they should be mimicked all the more for their efficiency. The diligent ants have the foresight to plan ahead as they gather food during the hot summer so they can survive the harsh winter, a business principle we are encouraged to match.

[26] The conies are but a feeble folk, yet make they their houses in the rocks;

The next example of creatures that are small but smart are the rock badgers or hyraxes. Their name in Hebrew, *shaphan*, literally "the hiders," showcases their wisdom; they are small and unwilling to expose themselves to danger, therefore they make their homes safe in rock crevices. They do not venture far from the security of their homes.

[27] The locusts have no king, yet go they forth all of them by bands;

Locusts are renowned for order and discipline since their members neither push another out of ranks nor crowd the rank next to them. Considering the order of the locust army, Jerome describes: "When swarms of locusts came…they flew in such order, by the disposition and command of God, that they kept their place like checkered squares in a pavement fixed by the hands of artificers; so as not to decline a point, nor even I may say a nail's breadth."

[28] The spider taketh hold with her hands, and is in kings' palaces.

The next example of creatures that are small but smart are not spiders but lizards (incorrect translation). Continuing the format, the first phrase gives an example of the animal's weakness: lizards are easy to catch. And the second phrase gives an example of their wisdom: lizards, in their search for delicious, pesky bugs, gain access to places most men never see, like the inside of kings' palaces.

[29] There be three things which go well, yea, four are comely in going:

In the last use of this idiomatic phrase, the author begins the sixth and final quaternion in verses 29-31, which is a list of things that wisely walk with a dignified stride and whose motion is majestic.

[30] A lion which is strongest among beasts, and turneth not away for any;

Lions are mentioned in over half (37) of the books of the Bible and are described as living in forests (Jeremiah 5:6), thickets (Jeremiah 4:7), mountains (Song of Songs 4:8), and desert places (Isaiah 30:6). The lion's whelp (LXX), the strongest of them all, mocks at fear and is not dismayed, neither does he turn his back from any enemy.

[31] A greyhound; an he goat also; and a king, against whom there is no rising up.

Continuing the list of things that walk or strut with wisdom is the animal that is well-knit in the loins, perhaps the rooster (not grey-hound), the male goat, and finally the greatest of them all, a king who leads his army into battle and cannot be withstood.

[32] If thou hast done foolishly in lifting up thyself, or if thou hast thought evil, lay thine hand upon thy mouth.

Verses 32-33 form the conclusion of the prophecy. Agur states that anger, whether it's being physically expressed or resides in your heart, can be averted through exhibiting extreme self-restraint or covering your mouth in shame (Job 21:5).

[33] Surely the churning of milk bringeth forth butter, and the wringing of the nose bringeth forth blood: so the forcing of wrath bringeth forth strife.

Agur uses the examples of churning milk and punching someone in the nose as illustrations of how anger can quickly convert a situation into something that is irreversible, an irreconcilable quarrel.

PROVERBS 31

[1] The words of King Lemuel, the prophecy that his mother taught him.

This instruction to King Lemuel, whose name means "belonging to God," begins with a superscription, the queen mother's direct appeal to her son. It continues with four pieces of advice before the section on the virtuous woman. These admonitions concern relationships with women, excessive drinking, mercy, and justice.

[2] What, my son? and what, the son of my womb? and what, the son of my vows?

The mother's oracle begins with a threefold question that underlines the earnestness of her teaching. Her child, perhaps "tender and only beloved in the sight of his mother" (4:3), was conceivably given by God, like Samuel, in answer to her prayers and vows.

[3] Give not thy strength unto women, nor thy ways to that which destroyeth kings.

The queen mother first admonishes the heir to the throne concerning relationships with women. She warns him not to overindulge or waste his vigor with too many women who can ruin him by turning his heart away after other gods (1 Kings 11:3-4).

[4] It is not for kings, O Lemuel, it is not for kings to drink wine; nor for princes strong drink:

The queen mother next admonishes her son concerning another temptation for kings, excessive drinking (1 Kings 20:16). Drunken rulers can only contribute to the downfall of a nation (1 Kings 16:9).

[5] Lest they drink, and forget the law, and pervert the judgment of any of the afflicted.

The reason for the warning is that it is not fitting for rulers to abuse alcohol because it causes them to forget what laws were decreed and thereby pervert justice toward their oppressed subjects (Isaiah 5:22-23).

[6] Give strong drink unto him that is ready to perish, and wine unto those that be of heavy hearts.

The queen mother advises her royal son to be compassionate by providing strong drink for those oppressed victims of society who are dying and cannot afford a sedative (Matthew 27:34), and to let the consumption of wine only be for those who are in anguish to make their heart glad (Psalm 104:15).

[7] Let him drink, and forget his poverty, and remember his misery no more.

The lives of such people are hopeless, so why not let them drink to the point of drunkenness so they may disremember their miserable lot in life and forget their troubles at least while they are drunk.

[8] Open thy mouth for the dumb in the cause of all such as are appointed to destruction.

The queen mother next advises him to pay special attention to the matter of justice and to become a powerful advocate for vulnerable members of society whose voice would otherwise go unheeded.

[9] Open thy mouth, judge righteously, and plead the cause of the poor and needy.

It isn't enough for a wise king to abstain from excess in regard to women and alcohol, but he must also exert his energy in a positive sense by speaking impartially for those who cannot speak for themselves. This ensures justice for those whom others seek to ruin.

[10] Who can find a virtuous woman? for her price is far above rubies.

Since women are often represented as the epitome of wisdom or folly, it is fitting the book ends with a description of what happens when you marry lady wisdom. Ruth is described as a woman of ability, a virtuous woman, and therefore a good wife (Ruth 3:11). The worth of the virtuous woman, who is rare and valuable, seems to depend on how successfully she keeps and increases the value of her home. The religious criterion for evaluating women seems to come as something of an afterthought (31:30).

[11] The heart of her husband doth safely trust in her, so that he shall have no need of spoil.

The husband of lady wisdom, personified in the virtuous woman, can trust in her knowing that she will greatly enrich his life both domestically and financially. The virtuous woman primarily represents the industry and domestic skills of a wise woman.

[12] She will do him good and not evil all the days of her life.

The virtuous wife is totally dedicated to honoring her husband. Everything she says and does is designed to enhance her husband's good standing in the slow-paced, tight-knit, and conservative ancient Jewish community.

[13] She seeketh wool, and flax, and worketh willingly with her hands.

Though she is rare, the description of her entrepreneurship suggests that Israelite women took an active role in business. This parable is typified in Lydia, "a seller of purple of the city of Thyatira" (Acts 16:14). Lydia was a merchant who sold the purple dyes to tanners, weavers, and others. The business of dyeing with which she was connected had long been centered in the city of Thyatira. Archaeological inscriptions have been discovered there that refer to a guild of dyers that was located in the vicinity.

[14] She is like the merchants' ships; she bringeth her food from afar.

The virtuous woman is frugal as she searches for opportunities of saving money by purchasing the home's goods cheaper at a distance from home, likely at the port. In doing this she would get the wholesale price and avoid the price markup at the market due to transportation of the goods there and the seller's percentage.

[15] She riseth also while it is yet night, and giveth meat to her household, and a portion to her maidens.

Since morning was the time for cooking, the grinding of grain was often done during the night, that is to say, in the early hours of the morning before the sun comes up. This is when the virtuous woman grinds enough flour to last one day and gives instructions to her servant girls.

[16] She considereth a field, and buyeth it: with the fruit of her hands she planteth a vineyard.

The virtuous woman knows how to multiply and compound her money. After inspecting a field and buying it from her own earnings, she determines the land is best suited for growing a vineyard instead of producing grain in order to maximize her return.

[17] She girdeth her loins with strength, and strengtheneth her arms.

She is energetic and strong as she employs great diligence in her work. Men in ancient times used to gird up their long and loose garments about their loins to move freely (Job 40:7), so metaphorically does the virtuous woman.

[18] She perceiveth that her merchandise is good: her candle goeth not out by night.

She is wise without—her business dealings produce great profits, and wise within—she knows not to light her lamps too soon in the evening since otherwise they would burn out in the darkness of night before the dawn. These lit lamps acted like a night-light.

[19] She layeth her hands to the spindle, and her hands hold the distaff.

She is never idling since her hands are busy spinning thread and her fingers twisting fiber. The ancient devices to spin thread were the hooked stick used as a spindle and the receiving stick was a distaff. They were usually made of wood, and few have survived from antiquity except as illustrated, for example, in Egyptian tombs.

[20] She stretcheth out her hand to the poor; yea, she reacheth forth her hands to the needy.

She is a compassionate woman and participates in the work of YHWH. The dividends of her investment in the poor are a promise that YHWH Himself will reward her for her good works (Deuteronomy 15:10).

[21] She is not afraid of the snow for her household: for all her household are clothed with scarlet.

Snow is rare in Jerusalem; less than ten times snow accumulated multiple inches during my 1,000 days of living there. When it snows, the virtuous woman is prepared and has no fear for her household because all of them are clothed in scarlet (literally "to shine or be bright") or warm clothing. This was the only way to keep warm in the winter besides having a fire. The rosy red faces of her family clothed with scarlet inside is contrasted with the cold, white snow outside.

[22] She maketh herself coverings of tapestry; her clothing is silk and purple.

The virtuous woman makes her own bedspreads and clothes. She dresses in the most honorable material (fine linen, see Genesis 41:42) and colors associated with royalty (purple gowns, see Esther 8:15). The virtuous woman dresses in a way reflective of her high social status.

The use of expensive things is not condemned but commended as rewards for her wisdom.

[23] Her husband is known in the gates, when he sitteth among the elders of the land.

She successfully enhances her husband's standing in the community as he takes his seat among the elders of the land. This was a prestigious, honorable, and serious responsibility that could not occur if his wife dishonored his reputation (Ruth 4:1).

[24] She maketh fine linen, and selleth it; and delivereth girdles unto the merchant.

Her business makes fashionable linen garments and sashes for cosmopolitan women (Isaiah 3:23) and sells them to the "merchant," or literally the "Canaanites," perhaps on the Philistine Coastal Plain, who would then export them to wealthy buyers abroad.

[25] Strength and honour are her clothing; and she shall rejoice in time to come.

The virtuous woman is confident in YHWH and her wise living. She is dressed with strength and dignity, which causes her to enjoy life to the fullest without any fear of what tomorrow may bring.

[26] She openeth her mouth with wisdom; and in her tongue is the law of kindness.

When she speaks, since she is slow to speak, her words, like those of the teacher of Proverbs, are full of wisdom and to be heeded. It is not only what the virtuous woman says but how she says it, with kindness.

[27] She looketh well to the ways of her household, and eateth not the bread of idleness.

She carefully watches over all the domestic affairs in her home. She is an entrepreneur (31:13) and a hard worker (31:17) who is frugal with money (31:14). She cooks for her family (31:15) and compounds her money (31:16), etc. In other words, she suffers nothing from laziness.

[28] Her children arise up, and call her blessed; her husband also, and he praiseth her.

The virtuous woman receives the highest respect and honor from those who know her best, her children and husband. When she enters the room, her children honor her presence by standing up and blessing her (Leviticus 19:32). Her husband also bears witness to her wise character in the concluding verses.

[29] Many daughters have done virtuously, but thou excellest them all.

Perhaps this conclusion can be regarded not only as the praise of the husband for his virtuous wife but also as the deduction of the author himself upon what happens when the young man marries lady wisdom.

[30] Favour is deceitful, and beauty is vain: but a woman that feareth the LORD, she shall be praised.

This book, which was written especially with the training of young men in mind, concludes with this warning. The book ends the same way it started (1:7), with the teacher's basic theme and the motto of the book, the essence of ancient Israelite philosophy, namely that the first step toward knowledge is having a reverential fear of YHWH.

[31] Give her of the fruit of her hands; and let her own works praise her in the gates.

The husband advises everyone in the most public of places, the gates of the city (1:21), to give the virtuous woman, the personification of wisdom, credit for what she has accomplished. Her achievements speak for themselves. It is what the virtuous woman does that makes her the fairest of them all.

Conclusion

As you have hopefully observed by now, the book of Proverbs is not just for inexperienced young people open to the influences of the world, but is just as much for the experienced parent or grandparent to study and apply. Finding the right answers to the problems life presents often demands more wisdom than the average person has. Solomon himself, speaking from experience, taught his children what his father David taught him—that getting wisdom is the principal thing to do.

The starting place for gaining wisdom is having a reverential fear of God (Proverbs 1:7). The individual proverbs further divulge that if people learn self-discipline, the right time to act, how to save money, the advantages of breaking free from the cycle of revenge, the necessity of speaking at crucial times and the folly of doing so in inopportune circumstances, and so on, they will give their parents tremendous joy and be well on their way to maturity.

I pray that this commentary has aided you, your kids, and your grandkids as you continue the lifelong journey of growing in the wisdom and knowledge of God's Word.

ABOUT THE AUTHOR

Prof. Tom Meyer earned a B.A. in Bible and Theology from Shasta Bible College in Redding, California. After this, he pursued biblical studies abroad. He moved to Jerusalem, Israel, where he earned two master's degrees from Jerusalem University College. During his 1,000-day stay in Israel and neighboring countries, he had such adventures as witnessing to Prime Minister Shimon Peres, sailing the Nile River, climbing Mount Sinai, and meeting his future wife, Sarah. Shortly thereafter, he began to present complete books of the Bible dramatically by heart as sermons. His unique gifting has made him the feature of numerous media interviews with outlets such as Fox News, Moody Radio, *The Jerusalem Post*, and more. Tom Meyer teaches at Shasta Bible College and speaks the Word of God dramatically from memory, including the entire book of Revelation, every Sunday in a different local church as a full-time ministry. He and his wife have four children.

ABOUT THE
INSTITUTE FOR CREATION RESEARCH

At the Institute for Creation Research, we want you to know God's Word can be trusted with everything it speaks about—from how and why we were made, to how the universe was formed, to how we can know God and receive all He has planned for us.

That's why ICR scientists have spent more than 50 years researching scientific evidence that refutes evolutionary philosophy and confirms the Bible's account of a recent and special creation. We regularly receive testimonies from around the world about how ICR's cutting-edge work has impacted thousands of people with God's creation truth.

HOW CAN ICR HELP YOU?

You'll find faith-building science articles in *Acts & Facts*, our bimonthly science news magazine, and spiritual insight and encouragement from *Days of Praise*, our quarterly devotional booklet. Sign up for FREE at **ICR.org/subscriptions**.

Our radio programs, podcasts, online videos, and wide range of social media offerings will keep you up to date on the latest creation news and announcements. Get connected at **ICR.org**.

We offer creation science books, DVDs, and other resources for every age and stage at **ICR.org/store**.

Learn how you can attend or host a biblical creation event at **ICR.org/events**.

Discover how science confirms the Bible at our Dallas museum, the ICR Discovery Center for Science & Earth History. Plan your visit at **ICRdiscoverycenter.org**.

P. O. Box 59029
Dallas, TX 75229
800.337.0375
ICR.org

THE BOOK OF BEGINNINGS

A Practical Guide to Understanding Genesis

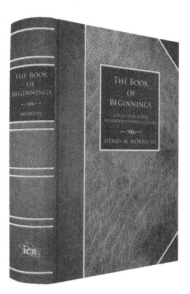

In this beautifully illustrated hardcover edition, Dr. Henry M. Morris III addresses the difficult issues in the Genesis record. These in-depth answers will give you confidence in your study of the Scriptures and help you communicate the richness of Genesis to those around you.

Find out about other creation resources at ICR.org/store

ICR.org

NOTES

NOTES

NOTES

NOTES

NOTES

NOTES